Night Benedictions:

365 Gentle Thoughts, Poems, and Meditations For the End of the Day

by Elizabeth Massie

Copyright Elizabeth Massie, 2014

Valley House Books

Cover art and interior art by Cortney Skinner
cortneyskinner.com

Printed in the United States of America

Dedicated to the Stars and Moon, the Stillness and Quiet, and all things that make up the Beautiful Night

Introduction

Most of us embrace the day. It's a time of doing, a time of seeing, a time of wakefulness and industry. We absorb its vitality, warmth, and light. During the day our five senses are kept active. We are keenly aware of what lies ahead of us, around us, and behind us. We are energized. We are busy, and our busy-ness keeps us focused.

Then comes the nighttime.

With nighttime, bedtime. Darkness. Stillness.

Some people struggle with the waning of the day and the arrival of night. They might have trouble sleeping or may fear or resent the presence of darkness, of stillness, of quiet. Thoughts that seemed productive and manageable in daylight seem determined to tangle themselves into uncomfortable knots as the Earth turns and the sun falls away. Though during the day we may have many friends, at night we may feel lonely, abandoned. An unbidden sense of hopelessness might rise up or a sense of being overwhelmed or defeated may press us down. Often we know these sensations aren't rational, but they are there, and they can be persistent.

Yet the nighttime is as much a part of our lives as day. It is as important and profound in what it has to offer. It gives us the chance to rest, and rest is critical to physical healing, mental acuity, and improved emotional and social functioning while we are awake.

I have found that a simple thought, poem, or meditation, read at bedtime, can offer a new way to envision and accept the night. A gentle saying about the inevitable, lovely darkness may help us understand the evening as the gift that it truly is, and allow us to embrace that gift.

The theme of these benedictions is consistent – the night is good and powerful, gentle and certain. This book is a compilation of passages, poems, and meditations that I wrote about nighttime over a period of a little more than a year.

With few exceptions such as illness, exhaustion, or being away from home, I created one each evening, sitting at my computer around 9:30 p.m. in the silent darkness and letting the thoughts, poems, or meditations come to my heart. I thought I would do this for a few weeks, posting them online to share with my friends. But then I kept going, feeling encouraged and relieved, discovering truths about the night and its precious offerings, and sensing a comfort in sharing them.

Here, then, is a years' collection of night thoughts. Read one each evening, silently or aloud to yourself or to a loved one who might find benefit. Read them front to back, back to front, randomly, or however you chose. Highlight the ones you like best to find and read again. It's your book; do with it as you choose. The readings can stand alone or be prelude to prayer or your own meditation. However you use this book, is my hope that these thoughts will be of comfort to you. May the peace of the night surround you. May it surround us. And may we sleep well.

About the Author

Elizabeth Massie is an award-winning author of a variety of works from novels, short fiction, and media tie-ins for commercial publishers to poetry, non-fiction, and fiction for educational publishers. She lives in the Shenandoah Valley with her husband, illustrator Cortney Skinner.

About the Illustrator

Cortney Skinner was born and raised in New England where his appreciation for classic painters and illustrators influenced his own art. Comfortable in either traditional or digital media, he is regularly called upon to create artwork and concepts for magazines, books and films. He lives in the Shenandoah Valley with his wife, writer Elizabeth Massie.

Evening 1.

Welcome, night. Greetings, darkness. The world has turned and your time has come again. We accept the quiet and rest you offer. As we lie down to sleep, may our thoughts become those of gratitude. May the last thing we dwell on be something wondrous from the day gone by. Something done for us or something we were honored to do for another. Something beautiful or sweet, touching or inspiring. Something large or small, something permanent or fleeting. May thankfulness ease our hearts and bring us the peace we need. The peace that embraces, the peace that heals.

Evening 2.

Day has faded into darkness.
Listen to the quiet.
Breathe the gentle stillness.
Feel the comfort of the night surround you.
As sleep approaches,
Close your eyes.
Think of someone you love dearly,
Someone near or far away.
 Send a wish his way
Or say a prayer for her.
For it is when we think lovingly of others
That peace will smile upon us
And enfold us.

Evening 3.

I see you, wondrous stars,
Peering through the ebony fabric of night,
Distant, brilliant representatives of
Eternity's most glorious light.
I feel you, wondrous soul,
Resilient through the struggles of the day,
Heart-close, brilliant entity that shines with
Eternity's most glorious light.
And now, under the canopy of the Universe and in the
Embrace of the Compassionate Divine,
Let go of your worries and release your uncertainties;
Accept the benediction of the gentle darkness
As it whispers, "Sleep well, dear one,
Sleep well."

Evening 4.

Ease into the night. Let the darkness and quiet mend what hurts and remind you how worthwhile you are. Sleep well.

Evening 5.

May the retreating daylight and arrival of night's soft shadows bring clarity of soul, comfort of heart, and a quiet certainty of purpose. Do not fret on the frustrations and fears of the day gone by. They are little more than chilly winds, stirring up the dust of doubts and clouding our vision. But those winds are past and gone; they are silenced and settled, over. Now, in this brand new moment, may your heart rise up in joy, embracing the fact that you are here, you are more capable than you knew, you can start again, and that you are loved. With this knowledge, sleep well. Sleep well and heal.

Evening 6.

Fireflies stitch the hem of ebony night
With delicate, silvered threads.
Night birds whisper within shadowed trees
As golden-eyed cats prowl stealthily through the grass.
I sit in in the darkness,
Gazing upward at stars that play at holding still,
Shifting so subtly that no human eye
Can detect their journey across the sky.
Yet on they go, cycling 'round and 'round.

Time will not be denied.
It moves to the rhythmic heartbeat of a universal clock.
Moment into moment.
Spring into autumn into winter into spring.
Days rising onto the scene, fresh, full,
Then stepping back to relinquish their holds
So that evenings shall have their turns.
A breeze whispers across the yard and I smile,
Thinking of friends who were here but then were gone,
Each one stitching the fabric of my life
With silvered threads of memories and joy.
Each rising into the scene with lessons and love
Then stepping away as they needed.

Time will not be denied,
So I embrace the warmth of day and cool kindness of night,
Accepting the rhythms of joy, sadness,
Stars, sunlight, morning, evening
All the better for friends both old and new,
For seasons that come and go.
For sweet sunlight and peaceful darkness that call me to rest.

Evening 7.

Thoughts frantic, thorny, relentless,
Barreling headlong into the encroaching shadows;
Can't run anymore,
Carry it anymore,
Do it anymore,
Bear it anymore.
But night is here;
Listen to the silence
Whisper in a voice felt in the heart
And recognized by the spirit.
You are not alone.
You are not weak.
You are weary.
Give in to the gift of sleep;
Let it lift
And hold you.
That is its divine mission;
This is its purpose.
Do not reject it or resent it.
Its strength will renew you.
Be at peace, then;
Be comforted.
Rest well, friend.
Good night.

Evening 8.

May the quiet beatings of your heart
Whisper you to sleep
While the sweet, silent moon keeps watch.
May your dreams carry you gently
From twilight to darkness to dawn,
And may you awaken to new wonders,
New hope,
New courage,
And a new and joyous clarity of purpose.
Good night.
Good night.

Evening 9.

What is done is done. What will come will come. But for now, the night waits, smiling, to give you rest. Sleep deeply. And may comforting, tranquil dreams be yours.

Evening 10.

The evening stars are still in the sky
Even when mist or clouds have hidden them.
The value of you is still there,
Even when you cannot sense it.
So now, as silent darkness enfolds you,
Release your doubts and uncertainties.
Be assured that no one is of greater value than you;
Your purpose is still unfolding,
And your strength is more than you might know.
With that simple truth,
Sleep deeply, friend.
Good night.

Evening 11.

Solitude;
Graceful, peaceful,
The moon, aloft and silvery-bright,
Alone but not lonely,
Content and secure with no need of accolade
For its purpose is enough.
Silent, satisfied,
Restful.
Solitude;
Quiet, peaceful,
Your soul, alive and wholly-bright,
Drawing in the gentle cloak of darkness
As a favorite blanket,
Soft, comforting.
Alone but not lonely,
Content and secure with no need of accolade
For its grand purpose is enough.
Be satisfied, then, and not fretful.
Be silent now.
Ease into the night and
Rest.
Dream.
Sleep.

Evening 12.

Night is here, whispering gently, spreading out her soft blanket upon the Earth. Release your worries to the sky; lie down and take comfort in the gift of rest. Let sleep renew your strength and heal your heart.

Evening 13.

When eyes are too tired to stay open,
Legs too weary to stand,
When arms are too spent to hold on
And minds too weary to brood,
Give in to the gentle embrace of night
Which is there to catch and to hold you.
Do not cling to today's fights
Nor wrangle with what lies behind you.
Exchange them for the tranquility of evening,
The healing peace of the darkness,
These moments of serenity.
Let your heart ease, your thoughts quiet,
And your soul nestle down into the sweet stillness.
Sleep well, friend.
Sleep well.

Evening 14.

The dark, still night has come again. Accept its powerful gift of tenderness. Surrender to the peace the darkness offers, a peace you well deserve. Let go. Give in. Be blessed. Be renewed. Sleep well.

Evening 15.

What is softness?
The whisper of a breeze,
Down of a chick,
Embrace of a friend,
Memory of a loved one,
Moon-glow on a field,
The sigh of the soul ready to sleep.
Receive the softness that awaits you
And rest well, friend.
Good night.

Evening 16.

The time has come to say good night. Peace to you, the true peace that comes with knowing you are worthy, loveable, and have something genuine to offer. And you are. And you do. Sweet dreams.

Evening 17.

The rhythms of the night call us.
Crickets and katydids sing within the trees,
Silent and then vocal,
Silent then vocal.
Waves slide upon the sandy shore,
Draw back
Then move forward again.
An evening breeze stirs the air,
Pauses, and stirs once more.
As the blessed darkness surrounds you,
Embrace the rhythm of your being.
Close your eyes.
Slow your breaths.
Breathe in love, breathe out fear.
Breathe in forgiveness, breathe out anger.
Breathe in reconciliation, breathe out worry.
Breathe in this moment, breathe out moments that came
before.
May this gentle rhythm carry you into sleep,
And may your sleep be deep and healing.

Evening 18.

Stars watch over you,
Moon smile down on you,
Trees stand guard for you,
Breeze whisper gently to you,
Darkness draw softly around you;
All that is good and kind,
Powerful and righteous,
Certain and loving and unfailing
Keep you until morning
And bless you with a soothing sleep.

Evening 19.

Lantern moon, glimmering stars,
Decorations in the vast, velvety ceiling of the sky.
"Come," they call, inviting your soul to
The slow dance of night where the rhythm
Is gentle and the pace is peaceful.
Darkness lifts you,
Rocks you gently to the music of your heart
And carries you into sleep.

Evening 20.

As quiet as fog and kind as a breeze,
Enfolding the city, caressing the trees,
Evening, so gently, comes 'round once more,
Bathing the windows, hallways, and floor,
Bidding bright sunlight a fond farewell,
Bringing pale moonlight and stories to tell.
Draw close, lie down, let wearied eyes close;
Release your sadness, worries, and woes.
Time now to rest and let healing begin
And find certain calm that resides within.

Evening 21.

The night may seem dark beyond dark,
And sadness heavy and cold,
Yet in the darkness the stars shine still and brightly so,
And still the warm light of goodness surrounds us
Offering its benediction of peace and healing.
Sleep well, friend.
Sleep well.

Evening 22.

Falling stars,
Leaping through night's eternal blackness,
Trailing brilliant, gossamer ribbons;
Happy to paint the sky in their moment,
To draw utterances of
Look! See!
Beautiful!
From those who look up from below.
We,
Wandering through life's uncertainties,
Have brilliance of our own,
To share, shine, and inspire in this, our moment,
To paint pathways of hope, courage, and peace;
To draw utterances of
Look! See!
Beautiful!
From those who wander with us,
Those who need us,
Those whom we need.

Evening 23.

May sleep's gentle arms keep you safe and enfold you with peace. Good night, friend. Sleep well.

Evening 24.

Throughout the long day we take hold, we lift, we grasp, we arrange and manage and toil. Now that sunlight has withdrawn and moved to places beyond, it is time to let the day be. It is time to be still and listen to the silence. The kindly night, fresh and new, reaches out to embrace, to comfort, to soothe. Let the sacred darkness do its job. Sleep well.

Evening 25.

In this moment of darkness,
This hour of deepest night,
Put aside the concerns of the day
And let go burdens that weigh you down.
Turn from that which spins and tangles
The heart and mind,
Digging relentlessly into the soul.
Be still;
Welcome the silence,
Breathe.
Healing will come with sleep,
And calm of heart,
Ease of mind,
Strength of spirit,
Peace of soul.

Evening 26.

Hold the hand of the night; let it lead you into calm tranquility. Trust, relinquish, surrender. May quiet enfold you, calm you, and reassure you that as you heal tonight, tomorrow you will stand strong.

Evening 27.

The soft blanket of darkness has come
To bring you rest.
Pull it up and around you.
Close your eyes.
Let your thoughts untangle and your worries fade away.
Listen to your heartbeats and your breaths;
Gentle companions, they will stay awake
And take care of things while you sleep.
Pleasant dreams, friend.
Good night.

Evening 28.

Put your cares down now. They will wait. Surrender and fall gently into the restful arms of sleep.

Evening 29.

Sun down, sun up, moon down, moon up.
Onward I go
Along life's rocky pathway.
Day into night,
Sights narrowed, looking ahead.
Frustrations, fears, struggles,
Goals to reach; hurry, hurry.

A sound catches me from somewhere beyond,
Within a lonely shadow of night,
A soft voice, calling.
I hesitate
Then slow, turn, and look.
Someone is there, seeking a smile, a kind word.
Someone forgotten, abandoned, lonely;
Hopeful eyes wide, deep.

My heart softens.
I reach out
And then see it is myself.
Myself seeking the love of myself,
The acceptance and compassion
I would give to others but withhold from me.

I embrace the fragile, precious soul waiting there.
I ask forgiveness and it is given.
Sun down, sun up, moon down, moon up.
At last we will sleep,
Together we heal.
We will have peace.

Evening 30.

Listen. Do you hear it? It is the beat of your heart, reminding you of the miracle you are. Listen. Do you hear it? It is the voice of the gentle night, welcoming you to rest.

Evening 31.

There is nothing that cannot be put down.
Our hands open as much to release as to grasp.
Let go of your cares.
Grant yourself a gentle rest.
The night speaks softly,
"Sleep now. Sleep, my friend."

Evening 32.

Every night, the vast, beautiful Universe opens to reveal its glory to us. It is a reminder that you are part of its eternal greatness even if feelings of insignificance try to tell you otherwise. Accept your place among it all. Embrace it. Breathe in the joy of that simple truth.

Evening 33.

Scarlet blaze above,
One last joyous, brilliant note,
And now, darkness. Peace.

Evening 34.

Sometimes at night,
In the soft, silent darkness,
Regret weighs on our shoulders,
Despair tightens our hearts, and
Worry dances behind our closed eyelids
Prodding, tormenting.
Yet the wearied regrets, despair, and worries that
Come at night
Are little more than specters,
Unmanageable phantoms that do nothing but
Spin frantic circles and tangle our spirits.
And so, like dust, let us shake them off.
Let us close our eyes, breathe the evening air,
And blow them away.
Let us claim our right to rest,
Our right to recovery, renewal, and healing.
In the morning, then, we will have the
Strength and clarity of mind to face what we need to change,
To manage what we need to manage;
Or we may well discover that the regrets, the despair,
And the worries were little more than mist
That has evaporated in the light of the sun.

Evening 35.

Evening,
A time to be still and become aware of the
Smallest, gentlest things.
The feel of cool sheets,
The warmth of your skin.
The scent of your pillow
And the faint trace of an earlier meal lingering round and
about.
The sounds of nocturnal creatures beyond the walls,
Of the clock ticking softly,
Of your own breaths and the
Hushed pulsing of your heartbeats at your temples.
The reminder that your are alive,
You are here,
And all shall we well.
Seek, then, the comfort that is offered,
The peace that waits for you to touch and embrace it.
Sleep well.
Sleep deeply.
Good night.

Evening 36.

Mindfulness brings increased gratitude. Gratitude brings increased happiness. Happiness brings increased peace. Tonight, as darkness swirls and settles around us, let us be aware of this quiet moment. Let our awareness bring thoughts of gratitude for who we are, where we are, what we have learned and have yet to learn, the struggles we have overcome and those we have yet to overcome, whom we love and who loves us. Whether we are thankful to God or the Universe or others in our lives, or are simply appreciative for our circumstances, let us be humbled. Let our gratitude open our hearts to happiness, and may our happiness usher in peace. Peace for a gentle and restorative night's sleep. Peace that carries into tomorrow.

Evening 37.

The night has drawn its curtain around you,
Gently calling you to turn your sights
From that which is beyond to that which is within,
That which is worthy, loveable, and wonderfully human.
Be still, be silent,
And let this simple, profound understanding
Rest easy on your mind.
Be at peace with yourself,
And in that peace, maybe your sleep be
Deep and your dreams sweet.

Evening 38.

With soft and silent hands
The night wipes clear the surface of the sky
To show us countless stars beyond,
Revealing the dark, deep, and unfathomably vast Universe.
And as we prepare to sleep,
We are humbled and comforted to be reminded yet again
That we are part of it all.
That we belong.
That we are connected.
That we are worthy of rest and peace that awaits us.
Good night.

Evening 39.

Take off the shoes of the day. Unlace them; kick them away with all the dust and frustrations, grit and fears that cling to them. Walk softly into the night, freed from those things that weighed on your heart and mind, ready, now, to rest. Ready, now, to slumber. Be certain that with sleep comes strength, clarity, and renewed confidence. Know that in the morning you will rise into yourself once more, filled with the goodness and power that is you, able to look challenges in the eye, able to face the world on your feet. Good night, friend.

Evening 40.

May the night be as kind to you as you need it to be. Sweet
dreams and a very pleasant sleep, my friend.

Evening 41.

As the gentle darkness of the night surrounds you, close your eyes and think back. Remember the smile you gave someone today, or the kind word. The door you held open for another person, or the helping hand you lent to someone with a heavy burden. The listening ear you offered. The patience you showed or the encouragement you gave. The glorious laughter or quiet sympathy you shared. Think back on that moment. You may have forgotten, but it is there. Recall that good thing you did and then sleep well. For each one of these actions is good and worthy. Each one is equal in its value and its power to help heal another as well as yourself. Sleep deeply, sleep soundly, for this is your reward.

Evening 42.

Let the noise of the day fade away.
Let the peace of the night flow in to take its place.
Be still.
Welcome the quiet.
Accept and surrender to the soft blessing of sleep.

Evening 43.

The world has turned again.
Day is done, evening returned.
The cycle continues.
Light and darkness,
Sounds and silence.
Motion. Stillness.
The cycle continues.
Worries fall away,
Hope flows in.
Sadness fades
Serenity enfolds.
Give in,
Accept,
Let go.
Find peace.
Sleep well,
Sleep deeply,
To arise when day has come again,
To arise, healed.
And the cycle continues...

Evening 44.

Freedom offers its hand to us at night. As daylight fades and shadows of evening sweep over the land, our lives slow down. It is then we find the time and clarity to consider those things that have held us down or tangled us up. Now, in the quiet darkness, is the moment to let go of anger or resentment, doubt or regret, and be free. It is the moment to forgive another or forgive yourself and be free. The moment to know that unjust criticism does not define you; let it go and be free. The moment to realize that doctrines or rules that are forced upon you and do not resonate with your soul's light are harmful; cut that cord and be free. Look inward and see the wonderfulness of you, the great potential and the worthiness. Breathe slowly, deeply, easily. Take the hand of freedom and feel its gentle, powerful joy move through you. Hold freedom close as you draw your blanket around you and nestle down to sleep. Know that in the morning, as the sun climbs from the depths into the sky, you will still be free. And so, rest well in your freedom. Good night, friend.

Evening 45.

Night is as perfect as day, the vanished sunlight as precious as the sunlight itself, the darkness a gift unlike any other. Be blessed with rest, and may your fear fade away and may peace rise up to take its place.

Evening 46.

Welcome the night as an old friend – comfortable, kind, quiet and patient. A friend who knows you as you are, who listens, comforts, and soothes. Who holds you gently as you offer up your consciousness to the silence of sleep, and stays with you until its time to awaken once more.

Evening 47.

Bands of blue
Brighten the sky,
Wash the lake,
Ride the mountain peaks,
Tint the twilight fog
Then disappear in the shadows of night.
Not gone,
Just resting,
Until it is time to shine again.
That which is, is.
You
Walk the road,
Ponder your pathway,
Face the world,
Stumble, rise,
Stand tall,
Take your struggles in hand,
Then put them aside in the shadows of night.
Still strong and courageous,
Welcoming rest,
Justified calm.
Peace rewarding.
Sleep now,
Until it is time to shine again.
That which is, is.

Evening 48.

Night is never absolute darkness. There are lights above. A silver sliver of moon. Distant yet brilliant stars. And when evening comes and melancholy seems too heavy and dark, be still, close your eyes, and find the light within. Like the moon, it is steadfast. Like the stars, it is brilliant. Do not despair, for your light will never burn out. Take heart, for it is more powerful than you can know. Rest with that certainty. And sleep well, friend.

Evening 49.

How endearing the sleeping child
In evening's embrace.
The dozing cat
By the fire,
The puppy curled up,
A furry bundle on the bed.
Vulnerable, innocent,
Precious.
So true for all of us, each and every one
When we give ourselves over
To the deepest rest,
And to dreams.
We are vulnerable.
We are innocent.
We are precious,
Cradled in the arms of night.
How wonderful, too,
To recognize these qualities in each other
Even as we awaken from our sleep
And face the new day.

Evening 50.

Restless soul, carrying burdens of both heart and mind,
Lay them down.
Night asks very little of you
But that you un-shoulder these weights
And accept the gift of rest.
Let gentle darkness hold your troubles,
Sort them for you,
And throw away those that are merely echoes and shadows,
So that when you arise
Not only are you renewed of strength,
But you will find your burdens greatly lightened.
Sleep well.

Evening 51.

When evening has come and sleep eludes, it is time to count.
Quietly. Steadily. Count the soft heartbeats deep within
yourself, purposeful, pure, and certain. Count your breaths,
slow and sure, a blessed rhythm of life. Close your eyes and
count the countless stars scattered across the night's sky of
your mind. Let your soul find peace in the gentle greatness of
eternity and its perfect cadence, for it knows you well. You are
part of it all. Count. Drift. Surrender. Sleep. Sleep, dear friend.

Evening 52.

Robert Frost wrote, "I have been one acquainted with the night. I have walked out in rain—and back in rain. I have out-walked the furthest city light…" Let us become acquainted with the night. Let's not fear, resent, or resist it, for it is as ancient as the world itself, as constant as sunlight and air, ocean and sky. It is the certain, gentle, and steady companion of every generation past and every generation to come. Let us gratefully accept the offerings of the night. Let us open our hearts and arms to welcome the peaceful power of its darkness. In that we shall become acquainted. In this the night will be our friend. And we will find rest.

Evening 53.

Silent hour, here again,
Softly drawing its dark veil around the bright day;
Urging us to rest
With a voice as tender as a caress,
As powerful as a rising tide,
As profound as a beating heart.
There is nothing to fear,
For the arms of evening are kind,
Forgiving,
Offering the chance to let go,
The chance to start over,
Relinquishing worries and regrets
To the breath of night
That will blow them, gently, away.
Sleep well.

Evening 54.

Brilliant stars,
Patterned across the blackness
In an eternal orchestration;
Each glowing point a note in
A glorious symphony
That is played by the imagination,
Known by the heart,
Embraced by the soul.
Let its music perform for you;
Let it enfold you,
Hold you,
And sing you to sleep.

Evening 55.

Evening ushers sunlight away, down the hillside,
Past the forest,
Out of sight.
Shadows reach out for one another,
Grasping hands across the field and town,
More shadows,
Then more still
Until, unified as one, darkness covers
Our world.
And though no bell calls us to rest,
No wind whispers "good night,"
We put down our troubles, our tasks,
Our missions.
Then, with lightened souls
And minds at ease,
We lie upon our beds within night's shadows,
And accept the wondrous gift of sleep.

Evening 56.

May tonight's dreams carry you on joyous, light-footed journeys away from the cares of the day. May you sing in your heart, fly with the moon, and dance beneath the black and starry sky. And all the while, may sleep's gentle hammock hold you tenderly, surely, until morning.

Evening 57.

Vast navy sky,
Pewter clouds
Scattered by a fragile, nocturnal breeze.
The forest, in dark silhouette, holds up the stars,
And the mountain lifts the moon
As if an offering of thanksgiving for this peaceful time.
The night landscape, painted by a Divine hand,
Is the backdrop for your dreams.
A sweet and wordless lullaby of nature
And of your own innate wonderfulness,
Sings you to a sleep
Well deserved.

Evening 58.

Surrender to the comfort of darkness,
The peace of stillness,
The soft beatings of your heart.
Claim this time to be silent,
To rest, to recover,
To heal and renew all that you are
And all you will offer the world on your rising.

Evening 59.

As I lie down to rest,
In the shadows of the night,
I consider the wonder of my hands.
Throughout the day they serve me,
Grasping, holding,
Reaching out to take what I need
And offering to others what I have to share.
No matter if they are old or young;
No matter if they are rough or scarred,
They are beautiful.
Evening is come, and for now our work is done.
We shall sleep well,
Peacefully,
And dream that we reach for eternity,
Grasp the stars,
And bring joy close to hold against our heart.

Evening 60.

Day has faded into the past; night has arrived once more, offering a quiet healing that comes with rest. For when we give up our consciousnesses and bodies to sleep, our brains remain busy, "taking out the trash," cleaning out toxic byproducts that accumulated during the day. What a wonder, what a gift this is. So do not resist the offering of the night, but surrender. Do not fight the need to sleep, but relinquish your grasp. Ease into the gentle darkness. It will hold you well and safely until morning.

Evening 61.

As I lie down
In the stillness of approaching night,
I consider the wonder of my shoulders.
Throughout the day they serve me,
Bearing the burdens of body, mind, and spirit,
Holding up against buffeting winds,
Keeping strong along steep pathways.
Then, when need be,
Willingly accepting the trials and worries of friends
And helping to share and bear them, too.
Now, as the west lays claim to the sun
And quiet darkness takes its place,
I prepare to sleep, un-shouldering the burdens of the day,
Knowing that in the morning
Many will be lighter for the rest,
While others will have faded away all together
Like fog in morning light.

Evening 62.

Listen to the darkness, calling to you with silent voice,
"Friend, put it all aside. Lie down and be at peace. Let the soft
blanket of sleep enfold you, hold you, comfort you. And I,
your partner of stillness and shadow, will sit with you until
morning."

Evening 63.

As I lie down to rest,
In the stillness of the night,
I consider the wonder of my feet.
Throughout the long day they serve me,
Humble, steadfast foundations
Bearing the weights of my life, its joys, worries, and duties
Along rutted roads, steep highways,
Moving me where I need to go,
Forward, onward,
Obeying demands even as they grow weary.
But it is time, now, to welcome gentle sleep.
Now we will travel only in our dreams,
Lightly,
Letting go of troubles
And fears,
Leaving behind rough pathways and steep roads.
It is time to fly forth into the darkness,
To sail free and joyous into the waiting sky.

Evening 64.

Even as breezes stir leaves into rustling whirlwinds along the ground and clouds into turbulent waves across the moon, even as your thoughts struggle with each other, revisiting issues of the day over and over again and creating turbulent whirlwinds of the mind, the Great Night calls you to rest. Let gentle sleep enfold you, draw you close, and ease your heart. There is no one more worthy of it than you. Believe this. There is nothing more true.

Evening 65.

Shall we walk together in our dreams, sharing thoughts that rise up from our hearts and souls, unencumbered and free? Shall we know answers that elude us in the business of the day, and then hold them on our waking? Yes, let's. And then, may we not be hesitant to share truths that we have discovered. For they are meant for us all.

Evening 66.

As I lie down to rest
In the stillness of the night,
I consider the wonder of my eyes.
Throughout the long day they serve me,
Observing bright sky, mountain peak,
Cityscape or wave-capped sea.
Studying the trail along which I travel
And the gentle faces of those
With whom I journey.
I see the vivid hues of life.
The glow of sunlight on leaf, on grass,
On distant clouds.
I witness the work of my hands,
The direction of my feet.
Onward.
And when day bids farewell,
Sunlight withdraws,
And darkness enfolds me,
I close my eyes to all that is beyond myself
And turn my sights within.
There I see the steady, bright light of my soul,
Serene and strong.
And when sleep comes,
It is peaceful.

Evening 67.

Breathe in the night, breathe out your worries. Accept the soft caress of silken shadows and gentle whispers of silence. Claim them, for it is yours. Sleep well and sleep deeply.

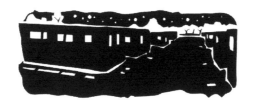

Evening 68.

As I lie down to rest
In the stillness of the night,
I consider the wonder of my arms.
Throughout the long day they serve me,
Encircling, embracing,
Releasing, setting free.
Carrying burdens both heavy and light,
Stretching out in expectation,
In hope,
Sometimes uncertainly,
Sometimes courageously.
And though they will not reach the moon,
They can reach others with ease
To offer compassion or
Encouragement.
Time now to rest;
Time to open the arms of my heart
And enfold the quiet darkness.
Time to sleep
And drift into tranquil dreams.

Evening 69.

Dark, eternal sky, our blanket,
Soft, comforting Earth, our bed.
Forgiveness, our pillow,
Peace, our lullaby,
And Sleep, the Blessed Reward
That humbles us, rebuilds us, and
Readies us for the day to come.

Evening 70.

As I lie down to rest
In the stillness of the night,
I consider the wonder of my ears.
Throughout the long day they serve me,
Conveying the sounds
Of loving voices,
Of music,
Of traffic and footsteps and phone calls.
They offer me warnings
Bring me comfort,
And teach me many things
When I truly,
Truly listen.
Now, evening has drawn its curtain around me
And it is time to be still,
To rest,
And to listen not to the world but, rather, to my heart;
To hear the still, certain voice that speaks softly within, saying
"Relinquish the trials of the day,
Accept the peaceful darkness,
And sleep well, dear friend.
Sleep well."

Evening 71.

Once more
Night has opened its door to you,
Revealing a welcoming place of rest,
Vast and starry,
Soft and silent.
Calling you in to shed the day,
To give in,
To let go.
To sleep
And sleep well.
To dream
And dream in the embrace of
Compassionate stillness.

Evening 72.

As I lie down to rest
In the stillness of the night,
I consider the wonder of my mouth.
Throughout the long day it serves me,
Allowing me to share words of encouragement,
To ask questions so I might know more than I did before,
To speak clearly what is important to me.
To take in nourishment,
To laugh, to mourn,
To sing, to cry,
To sigh and soothe others with gentle sound.
Evening is here and the time to be quiet has come.
I close my eyes to rest
And the voice I hear is that
Of my soul as it whispers to the Eternal.
For we are friends of the closest kind,
Knitted together, inseparable, fearless,
Speaking softly,
Singing songs of peace and hope
And certainty.
Sleep well.
Sleep well.

Evening 73.

Night is here. Find your favorite pillow, favorite blanket, favorite partner, or favorite pet, and snuggle up. Because nighttime, sleep time, should be the coziest time of all.

Evening 74.

As I lie down to rest
In the stillness of the night,
I consider the wonder of my legs.
Throughout the long day they serve me,
Carrying me to places I want to go,
Bravely, perhaps, or hesitantly,
Determinedly at times, or cautiously.
Climbing, hiking,
Walking, dancing;
Standing strong when need be,
Allowing me to sit when strength is spent.
Now time has come to rest,
To sleep in gentle shadows.
I am still,
There is peace.
And in my dreams I will climb
To the stars and dance with the moon.

Evening 75.

Do not worry over the day,
What was done or left undone.
You have taken on your tasks and
Accomplished what you could.
All is well.
Tomorrow will wait.
Now, be in this moment.
Put down the past and accept the present,
This moment,
This night,
These gentle shadows.
Allow yourself the sleep they offer.
Be kind to yourself, for
All is well.
Tomorrow will wait.

Evening 76.

There is nothing of the night to fear but your own doubts and regrets; lie down in quiet, cover yourself in gratitude, and may your sleep be sweet and peaceful.

Evening 77.

As shadows tumble, fall, and gather, weaving together the serene darkness of night, take with you to bed your gratefulness. Remember something good from the daylight hours, something kind said, a favor done, a smile offered. Recall the scent of a breeze, the touch of a hand, the sound of footsteps of someone you love. Think back, hold the memory close, ease your breaths, and sleep well.

Evening 78.

Evening comes on,
Quietly, unobtrusively,
Brushing away the noise and
Struggles of the day,
Offering a soft place to rest.
Come, now;
Accept the serenity of evening.
Open your heart and mind to the peace.
Brush away your worries and regrets,
Fears and struggles.
Take it in,
Sleep deeply,
And fly on the soothing wings of gentle dreams.

Evening 79.

The night does not shy away from us when we are sad, but covers us and gives us time to be still, to be quiet, to grieve, to pray, to wonder, to accept life's difficulties. Pull close the gentle shadows and be in the moment. Sleep will come, and when it does, it will help heal the battered heart. Good night, friend. Good night.

Evening 80.

Evening reaches out to carry us gently beyond the bustling realm of golden day and into the silent, silvered shadows of night. Here, surrounded by the dark and peaceful quiet, take time to think back on those you encountered today. Think of the tender kindness you shared with someone who was sad. Think of the patience you offered to someone who struggled. Think of the understanding you felt toward someone who was overwhelmed. And now, turn that toward yourself. Feel the kindness, the patience, the understanding. Do not reject or deny them. Accept them, for they are given to you with as much love as you gave others. You are worthy. It is good that you are here. It is good that you are. Know the gratitude others feel for you. Now sleep. And may your dreams be sweet.

Evening 81.

Even if you cannot see the moon,
The swirling night clouds,
Or the gossamer threads of the Milky Way
Against the blackened sky,
They are there.
Even when you feel removed or alone,
Isolated in the shadows of evening
And cannot sense a connection
Or see the faces of those who care,
They are there.
Darkness is but an absence of light,
Not an absence of love or friendship,
Courage or strength.
When you put down your tasks to rest
And close your eyes
You lose nothing that is good or real or whole.
That which is, is,
Whether in the light of the noon sun or the
Gentle glow of the evening stars.
Breathe in the powerful peace of reality,
Of certainty, of hope,
Of comfort.
Good night.

Evening 82.

As much a part of sea as sky, of valley as mountain, of sun as rain, of wind and calm, of night and day, and equal to them all, are you. You are here. Precious. Justified. And with this certain knowledge, shed the insecurities that cling to you. Let go the doubts that fear, in its selfish ignorance, demand you keep close. Open your hands, your mind, your soul to find the stillness that awaits. Let the evening surround you and hold you. Accept the peace that is offered, the peace that was always there. Sleep well, friend.

Evening 83.

Winking star,
Rustling tree,
Glowing moon,
Darkening hillside,
Stirring breeze,
Whispering grass,
Drifting cloud,
Barking fox,
Singing owl,
Purring cat,
Ticking clock,
Beating heart,
Resting spirit.
Good night, dear friends.
Sleep well.

Evening 84.

Think back on the day. Recall the joys, the challenges, the struggles and successes. Most importantly, think back on those to whom you were kind. To those you gave a smile, an encouraging word, a helping hand, or patience when it was needed. When you have remembered this, release your worries to the gentle arms of the night. Then rest, assured that your deed was good. Sleep well, knowing that good deeds, like starlight, shine far and wide in all directions.

Evening 85.

Night is not the death of day,
Nor day the death of night,
Light does not destroy the dark
Nor dark destroy the light.
Stars will shine through gentle night,
At day, in turn, the sun
Will smile upon the precious Earth
Until her work is done.
Dreams arise from that which is,
What is evolves from dreams,
Both sleeping and awake we
Travel life's unending streams.
Don't resist the hour to wake,
Nor fight the hour to rest,
Sure it is that each is right,
Each, in time, is best.
This, the moment, shadowed,
Silent, peaceful, calm, and deep,
Holds out its hand, for now's the time
To welcome blessed sleep.

Evening 86.

Study the night, the quiet, the darkness,
And in this learn that it is good.
Put away any trepidation of it
And come to know its beauty and purpose.
Come to know the treasure that it is.

Evening 87.

An evening fire, more brilliant because of the darkness.
The darkness, deeper because of the fire.
Such is the day, more dear because of the night,
And the night more lovely because of the day.
Each, in turn, right and good.
Let us embrace this night.
Welcome the rest, the peace, and the calm that it brings.
And may our sleep be deep, dear, and lovely.

Evening 88.

The voice of the evening is understanding, the song of the shadows is gentleness, the breath of the night is forgiveness. Embrace them all, and let them in, for they are meant to reside in your heart. Open your heart and release your troubles; fall into the gentleness of sleep well-deserved. Strength and healing come with rest. And when the sun rises, rise, too, and offer understanding, gentleness, and forgiveness to those who share the day with you.

Evening 89.

Shadows touch shadows,
Darkness clasps darkness.
Stars hold hands across the
Universe's indigo-black canvas
And the moon reaches out for the Earth.
The night beckons with gentle hands
To come, lie down, and rest.
Gathering all together,
Close,
Comforting,
A convergence of sweet silence,
Of restoration,
Of harmony,
Of sleep.

Evening 90.

We ask our weary and anxious hearts,
When shall things change?
When does despair become hope
And uncertainty become truth?
When does fear become understanding
And failure fall away to reveal
A clear and solid path?
The answer is quiet and sure,
Whispering on the night air
In a voice as gentle
As evening starlight,
"In a moment, it shall.
A moment is all that is needed
For a transformation of mind or soul;
A transformation that steps in from outside,
Or wakes inside to shine outward.
Startling or familiar,
But always renewing."
Therefore do not let troubles steal sleep away,
But rest assured that change is as certain
As sunset,
As sunrise.
Each second is new,
And coming daybreak, you will rise into that newness.
You will step into that moment.

Evening 91.

Do not fight to stay awake
As darkness comes;
Just as tides roll in and out,
As summer releases its hold to autumn,
Autumn to winter,
Winter to spring
To summer again,
Day and night, in turn,
Take their proper places upon the Earth.
You, child of the Earth, are
Meant for the tides,
The seasons;
You are meant
As much for song as silence,
For frivolity as introspection,
For daytime and eventide.
Find peace in knowing how much a part
You are of it all,
And welcome evening's kind offering
Of rest.
Sleep well, my friend,
Sleep well.

Evening 92.

Watchful moon,
Gentle breeze,
Candle-stars,
Hearts at ease.
Music drifts
Through soul and mind,
Joyful respite
Here to find.
Darkness whispers,
Shadows sing,
Peaceful, healing
Sleep they bring.
Grateful spirit,
Quiet thought,
What is needed,
What is sought,
Comes in softly,
Gentle, sure,
Gift of wholeness,
Sacred, pure.
Breath of hope,
Thankful sigh,
Blessed rest
Beneath night's sky.

Evening 93.

Sweet evening surrounds you,
Stars hold high above you,
And the gentle, golden watchman
Accepts his sacred duty in the black, sea-vast sky.
Release the day now, and ease into the night.
If you must hold onto a thought as you melt into the warm
embrace of sleep,
May it be a memory of goodness,
Of something kind or beautiful,
compassionate or forgiving,
Tender or amazing or loving you experienced during the day.
Shake off the ragged, torn thoughts that overwhelm or
depress;
Throw them away.
They are done and over.
Train your heart toward the good,
And its profound power will comfort, soothe and heal you.
Rest, then.
And be well.

Evening 94.

Sometimes the day seems overwhelming;
It feels as if others we pass on the street
In the store or on the highway
Have answers we don't.
We see confidence and ease,
Smiles and lighthearted expressions
That hint of goals at hand,
Dreams accomplished,
While we trudge on, looking down rather than ahead,
Our rhythms plodding,
Hearts fatigued,
Hopes faded.
Yet remember that no one is without a struggle.
Every soul has rough lands to cross,
Mountains to climb;
Even the hottest desert gives way to field and forest.
A blistering sun surrenders to the cool kindness of stars.
Therefore, as night welcomes you
Tenderly, gently into its fold,
Accept it.
There is restoration to be found in sleep,
And recovery in rest.
Deny your worries, put them down,
Let the evening give to you its gifts
And let the darkness renew your strength.
You will heal.
And you will rise in the morning
With renewed determination,

Creativity, hope,
Ready for new pathways to take,
Highways to explore,
Goals to reach.
Sleep, now.
Sleep, friend.
And find the peace you deserve.

Evening 95.

Brilliant light,
White to butter cream,
Translucent, pale,
To shimmering sherbet orange,
And vivid scarlet,
Shifting again to
Indigo,
Shadowed sapphire,
To silvered slate,
And the sacred,
Perfect black of night.
Blink.
Silvered slate to
Sapphire and indigo,
Scarlet and shimmering orange
To butter cream,
White,
And the brilliant, beautiful
Light of day.
Blink.
Begin again.
The circle turns,
The pendulum of Earth swings gently,
Perfect rhythm of time and life.
We rise,
Expand into the day,
Move and create,
Love and struggle,
Slow,
Close
To rest.

Blink.
Begin again.
Feel the connection,
Know you are as much a part of
This rhythm as
The rising and dimming sun,
The swelling, diminishing night.
Breathe it,
Feel it,
Grow into it and from it;
Take of it and
Give of it.
Day to night to day
To night.
Sleep deeply
As well you should
For your rightful place.
Dream peacefully
And be restored and ready.
Blink.

Evening 96.

"Be still," whispers the wind.
"Evening comes, bringing rest."
"Quiet now," echo the stars.
"Breathe in the silence and calm."
The moon sighs, smiles,
And the darkness speaks in a voice
So soft that only the soul can hear its appeal.
"Feel the arms of night around you,
Sense the peace that embraces you.
Surrender to sleep's gentle and certain power,
To restoration,
Renewal,
Healing."
Quiet now, my friend.
Be still.
Breathe in the silence
And the blessed calm.

Evening 97.

Night waits patiently for you to settle in,
To still the light,
To release the breath you've been holding
And put down the burdens you've been shouldering.
Draw in the quiet and the calm;
Surrender to the gentleness of evening shadows.
Turn all things over to That Which Is
And to That Which Shall Keep You
And hold you tenderly until morning.
Sleep well.
Pleasant dreams.

Evening 98.

Here is the night,
Kind, gentle,
Clothed in pewter, navy, and deepest ebony;
Greeting you with open arms
And singing,
"Welcome to this, my time.
Find your place here, my dear friend.
Rest your head and I will tell you stories
Of joy, of hope, of newness, and peace."

Evening 99.

Is there anything more profound than the sky at night?
Drawn open to reveal a satin-black eternity set with countless glistening stars
And faint, chalk-dot galaxies of unfathomable size and unimaginable distance?
Yet never forget that this vast canvas is not separate from us,
But we are in its midst and we are a part of it.
Humbling and sobering, this truth.
Uplifting and joyous, this reality.
Do not be proud, then, but be grateful.
Do not be downcast, but be assured and comforted.
You are as meant to be as the planets and moons,
As the solar winds and bright comets.
Small in size but unfathomable in your abilities to create, to heal, to help, to love. Consider your place.
Embrace your purpose.
And sleep well, sleep peacefully, in the sureness of it all.

Evening 100.

As the curtains of day draw closed,
As light fades and darkness
Assumes its rightly place across the Earth,
Let your worries fade;
Let serenity assume its rightful place
In your heart.
Close your eyes
And choose the one word that
To you
Is the most beautiful,
The most powerful in its tranquility.
Perhaps the word is Love.
Or Hope.
Or God,
Or Mercy,
Forgiveness,
Joy,
Or Kindness.
This is your mantra;
This will lead you to rest.
Breathe slowly, easily,
And with each inhalation
Whisper the word silently to your soul,
Then exhale.
Inhale, whisper silently, exhale.
Inhale
Whisper
Exhale.

Feel the rhythm;
It is the rhythm of peace,
Of spirit,
As pure as the rhythms of
Days to nights and nights to days,
As tides and seasons
And snows to rains to sunlight,
And the beating of your heart from moment to moment.
Give in,
Surrender,
And sleep.
Sleep well.

Evening 101.

As evening settles around you, let your mind go quiet, and find appreciation for who you are and where you are. The spinning wheels of anxiety are no match for the gentle power of thankfulness, and tangled thoughts of frustration become unknotted in its steady fingers. Breathe in the reality of goodness. Recall the love. Remember the kindness. These good things remain and do not change. They surround you; they await your acknowledgement, your acceptance. In that simple act of appreciation, the beautiful darkness of night is free to wash away the painful darkness of despair. And then, with a lightened heart and spirit relieved, sleep well, sleep deeply, sleep peacefully.

Evening 102.

Light softens.
Sounds quiet.
Day fades into night, relinquishing its hold,
Trading off, stepping back,
Bowing its head in honor of the encroaching darkness.
Night steps in and with jeweled fingers lifts the stars
Against the black canopy,
Raises the white moon to its rightful place
And nods gently at the world below.
In the softened quiet, find your rightful place.
Draw the peace around you;
Let the sweet weariness encircle you.
Now sleep, dream,
And be comforted.

Evening 103.

River of life,
Flowing steadily through the forest of time,
Twisting, turning,
Tumbling, churning,
Singing, sighing,
Flowing, flying over stones,
Through shallows,
Unstoppable, determined in its journey.
Slowing, easing,
Warming in the dappled sunlight,
Freezing in the grip of winter's frosted breath.
Dawn-break, daylight,
Twilight, midnight,
Quieting, whispering,
Onward, renewed.
We are rivers of life,
Each of us moving steadily through the forest of time,
Unstoppable, determined in our journeys,
Turning, twisting,
Steady, listing, flying,
Slowing, easing,
Twilight, midnight whispering,
Quieting within pine-scented shadows,
Beneath moon-lit boughs.
Sleep now;
Regain life's energies
For your journey as it continues,
Dawn-break, daylight,
Onward,
Renewed.

Evening 104.

At this very moment,
Stars blaze in infinite numbers,
Joyously throughout the Universe,
Planets continue their appointed courses
Around our glorious sun;
The glistening moon encircles the Earth,
And the seas crash against countless sand-painted shores.
Winds stir lakes, leaves chase each other along
A river's meandering pathway,
Songbirds settle in branches;
Owls awaken to watch, listen, prowl.
Spiders cease their spinning;
Cats curl up on blankets,
And dogs stretch out on beds.
Now, in this very moment, sleep offers to you its kind hand,
Its welcoming embrace.
Do not dwell on what is to come,
What is left undone,
What seems incomplete or misunderstood.
Do not deny this moment its blessed purpose.
Find the joy of simply being.
The joy in rest,
The joy in renewal.
And sleep well, friend.
Good night.

Evening 105.

Starlight, moonlight,
Candlelight, lamplight,
Burning brightly in the blackness;
Partners with the night.
Heart light, soul bright,
Rising up with perfect sight
Flying joyously, freely, through the darkness;
All is well, all is right.
Good night.
Good night.

Evening 106.

When the need for sleep arises, do not fight it. There is no battle here, no foe to defeat. The night is your ally, the darkness your friend; they come whispering gently, with compassion and understanding. Acknowledge them, welcome them, the night, the darkness. Open your heart and discover that the night is as much a part of you as the day; the darkness is as lovely as the light. To be well you must rest well. Give in, then, to the kindly night. Surrender to the peaceful, tender darkness. There is nothing to lose. There is much to be gained. Sleep well, friend. Sleep well and heal.

Evening 107.

Even on the darkest of nights, do not be afraid. Even when all things seem hidden and vanished within the black veil, there is a light to guide you. You may be overcome with sorrow. You may be worn down and weary. Rest, then, friend. Sleep beneath the silent midnight sky. And trust that when you awake, even if the morning seems dark still, the light remains. For it is the light that is your soul, burning steadily and surely, offering comfort and peace. Ready to show you the way.

Evening 108.

The evening moves in quietly,
Crossing the lake,
The field,
The farms,
Rolling up the roads, an ebony mist,
Through the towns,
And into the cities,
Encouraging the sunlight to travel onward, away,
Then taking its rightful place
For the time it is given.
Silent it lies, and still,
A vast and gentle cloak upon the world.
You are surrounded by this night.
You are enfolded by its kindness.
Slow your mind,
Your anxious heart;
Put aside your worries.
What is, will wait.
What is not, let go.
Close your eyes,
Lie in the stillness.
Let peaceful emptiness fill you,
Let silence hold you,
And just be.
Be in this time you are given.
Be in this place where you lie.
Be the breath,
Be the heartbeat.
Know the stillness of the evening.
Accept the comfort of its blessed darkness.

Evening 109.

That night is half of life.
May we see it for what it is,
Beautiful and endearing,
Certain, gentle, cleansing;
Ready to offer rest,
Healing, strength,
And peace to us all.
Good night, dear friend.

Evening 110.

Night, friend for life,
Has come.
Let your eyes close,
Your breathing ease,
Your thoughts soften.
Do not fret over things past
That are not of your doing;
The fabric of the day gone by
Is not yours alone.
All the threads are not of your weaving,
To manage or untangle.
Free yourself of residual worries;
Release them to your friend, the night.
What you will do tomorrow, you will do.
For now, be gentle to your soul,
Be kind as the evening is kind.
Let your eyes close,
Your breathing ease,
Your thoughts soften.
And sleep deeply.
Sleep well.

Evening 111.

Race run, vanished sun,
Day's done.
Soft bed, shadows fled,
Fears shed.
Dark sky, comfort nigh,
Hearts sigh.
Hope keep, drifting deep,
Sweet sleep.

Evening 112.

Starlight's gentle glow,
Earth, in shadows, lies below.
All of us, a part.

Evening 113.

Do you hear the song of the wind, the whisper of the stars, the voice of the moon? Do you feel the gentle breath of darkness, the touch of stillness, the caress of the moment? They have come to you. They know you, as you know them. Shed your fears; toss your worries into the past. Open your heart; close your eyes. Draw down beneath the soft blanket of the night. Find comfort there. Find healing. Dream peaceful dreams, my friend. Sleep well.

Evening 114.

Fading sun and rising night,
Shadows, twilight, vanished light,
Perfect darkness, still and whole,
Gentle comfort for the soul.
This the rhythm, steady, sure
With its certain, kind allure.
Put the dusty day away,
Evening now shall have its say.
Gift of quiet, healing peace,
Claim the offer of release.
In the arms of nighttime, rest,
Spirit now profoundly blessed.
Stars above will gently keep
And hold you as you drift to sleep.

Evening 115.

Follow the night into the darkness; it will guide you by the
cheerful shining of the stars and the smile of the silver moon.
Let your worries fall away; you are now, not then. You are
here, not there. Dance into your dreams. Sing, fly, and be
caught up in joy. Open your arms, your heart, your spirit.
Breathe in the freedom! And when you awaken, take it with
you as you follow the morning into daylight. Share your joy
beneath the beaming sun.

Evening 116.

The lovely night,
Self-assured and gentle,
Calls you to rest
In her vast and comforting arms.
Relinquish,
Surrender,
Let go and drift into peaceful dreams.
Sentinel stars will watch over you,
Drifting clouds will smile down on you,
And that which is Eternal will swirl around you,
Whispering to your soul
That you are known,
You are blessed,
You are loved.
And in that certainty,
Sleep well.
Sleep deeply.
Good night.

Evening 117.

Tired, burdened, worried,
We carry on,
Shoulders strained beneath troubles,
Fears, and tasks incomplete.
But know that
The night was made for this moment,
For this time of weariness;
The turning of the earth
From the sun,
The drawing of the
World's grand curtains,
The dimming of the sky
And rising of distant,
Pin-point stars.
This is the place of rest,
This is the time for sleep.
Silenced by darkness,
Softened by moonlight,
Cradling all within a gentle sigh.
Good night.
Rest well.
Be healed.

Evening 118.

Worries seek out the night; they rise up brasher, louder, more tangled, more determined than in the light of day. Though unwanted, they settle in gleefully as if invited, feeding on the silence, savoring the darkness. Yet wait. Consider. Are not hopes as real as worries? Are they not as justified as anxieties, and even more so for the comfort and courage they offer? They, too, seek out the night, though we find ourselves bullied by worries and surrender to their angry demands. Shake your anxieties away. Toss them aside. Then, in the silence of the blessed night, welcome hope. Let your heart find the peace it offers. Let your mind ease with the calm contentment it brings. And sleep well, friend. Sleep well.

Evening 119.

The evening does not judge;
The moon does not weigh nor condemn.
The stars are in the moment,
Shining without hesitation or consideration.
Be like the evening,
The moon,
The stars.
Put away judgments and condemnations.
Listen.
Hear the distant train,
The owl,
The breeze.
Feel the coolness of air,
The softness of a pillow.
Sense your heartbeats,
Your breaths.
Find the profoundness of
That which is.
And with that wondrous awareness,
That warm, certain nightlight
Within your soul,
Drift to sleep.
And sleep most peacefully.

Evening 120.

Do not resent the night; she is the dear sister of the day, clothed in stars and velvet darkness. And she holds a smile for us all, and peace to those who will accept it.

Evening 121.

What is there to fear as day gives way to night? All that is there was there; nothing rises in shadow that was birthed from shadow. Evening is as beautiful as afternoon, midnight as worthy as midday, twilight as lovely as dawn. The rhythm of the world is the rhythm of life, echoed in our heartbeats and our breaths, known by our souls. Relax into the night and sleep as the rhythm of life carries you gently forward and the peaceful shadows keep watch. And rest well, friend.

Evening 122.

Night is here once more,
A welcome friend, steadfast,
Certain,
Profound.
Find the peace and realization
That is offered in this evening's moment.
Close your eyes;
See within yourself the great, dark sky.
Rise up into the blackness,
Float among the stars, the moons, the planets.
Witness the flaring comets,
Swirling nebulae,
Grand spiraling galaxies,
And embrace the glorious vastness around you.
Be assured that you are not apart
But part of it all.
You belong.
You are rightfully here on this Earth,
In this galaxy,
In this Universe.
You move with the rhythm of all that is;
You are a melody in the symphony of eternity.
And now, in this kindly night
Sleep soundly,
Sleep well,
Sweet dreams.

Evening 123.

The light of day fades; the dust of our works settle. Shadows of night reach out for one another, coming together silently, weaving a blanket of calm, of peace, so that we may rest. Rest then, friend. Sleep well. It is needed. It is deserved.

Evening 124.

Consider the moon,
The gold-hued eye
That holds steady and unblinking
Against the black canvas of night.
There is no challenge in its Earthward gaze,
No request, no demand.
No judgment or reprimand.
The light it reflects is certain yet gentle,
Silent,
Calm.
Close your eyes now
And let the moon keep watch.
Close your eyes now,
And let the gentle,
Calm,
Certain Light
Of your soul ease you into sleep.

Evening 125.

This is a night of
Miracles.
The incomprehensible vastness of the sky,
Black against black;
The brilliance of stars,
The silent, drifting moon.
A stillness and quiet
That hums with
Life;
Breaths on the air,
Heartbeats in rhythm with others around the
Earth.
Thoughts turned inward to the vastness of the spirit;
Hope, renewal,
Expectation and awe,
All within reach
Within each moment.
This is a night of miracles,
For existence is a miracle,
Hope, a miracle.
Renewal,
Expectation,
Joy,
Love,
Potential,
Forgiveness,
Compassion,
And Love,
All miraculous, all wonderful,
Whether understood as Divine or secular.
And as the world rotates toward another day,

Know that
Tomorrow night, too,
Shall bring a night of miracles.
And all nights to come,
For all that is real,
For all that is offered and given,
For all that is already ours.

Evening 126.

Beneath the beautiful star-lit sea,
Release your worries, let them be
Embrace the stillness and be free,
Rest,
Sleep,
Heal.

Evening 127.

The sun fades, the stars awaken, and the darkness rolls in, surrounding us like a silent mist, a gentle cloak, peaceful and comforting, drawing us down and away from the cares of the day. In this quiet smallness let us be aware of that which the sun's bright light may have hidden from us. The simple things, insightful things. The rhythm of our heartbeats. The certainty of our breaths. The sense of our hand within our hand, the awareness of another nearby who loves and needs us. The knowledge that we are part of all there is, and our purpose has not given up on us. Rest, sleep, recover. Tomorrow, rise and step forward into the next moments of your life with simple and profound certainty.

Evening 128.

The night has come 'round again.
Pause in your journey.
Put down your burdens,
Un-shoulder your cares;
Sit beneath the moon and
Savor the sacred silence.
Warm yourself beside the
Golden, dancing fire of
Goals met
And dreams yet to grasp.
Then, content with what was,
What is, and what will be,
Lay yourself down.
Feel peace enfold you;
Hear the whispered song of the Divine,
"Sleep well, beloved.
I will watch over you.
Sleep well."

Evening 129.

The darkness, whole.
Moon and stars lack nothing
And the world has all it needs.
Animals that sleep or creep within darkness,
Trees standing in the stillness of midnight,
Rivers rushing rocky beds, feeling their ways
To the seas in the faint evening-glow,
And ocean waves crashing over and again,
Tossing salty starlight in an ecstatic offering to the sky;
Are all whole, complete, and right.
So are we,
Children of Creation,
Complete and lacking nothing.
Emptiness is perception,
Sad and oppressive,
Springing from weariness and fear and the
Unsettling, fretful dusk of the mind.
Quiet now, friend.
Draw the healing blanket of night around you
And let go bleak imaginings.
Realize that which the rivers know,
And the stars and seas,
And animals, moon, and trees.
All you need is in you, surrounds you;
You are right,
You are whole.
Breathe deeply, feel this truth
Then lift a joyful offering from your soul,
And sleep well.
Sleep well.

Evening 130.

Evening arrives silently, covering all it touches with gentle darkness. Some fear the night, and reject it. They shine anxious, glaring lights to chase the night away. But let us not be distressed. Let us acknowledge the beauty and power of evening and accept it with a thankful heart. For night is as true and good as day, and sleep is as good and true as wakefulness. Each a perfect gift in its time. Now that the stars have climbed to their appointed places and the moon has settled in the black-cloak heavens, let us relinquish our cares and ready ourselves to rest. To breathe, and breathe wholly. To sleep, and sleep deeply. And may the dreams that be, be peaceful.

Evening 131.

Much we have never seen, much we may never know, yet the night, the moon, the distant points of stars, all converge to give us a time to rest, to dream, to heal, and in healing rise to see more, to know and understand all the more.

Evening 132.

A new night moves in gently,
Gathering up all colors from the land
And tucking them away
Until later,
So that now, nothing appears more
Brilliant than another,
Lovelier than another,
More important than another.
The new evening arrives,
Wiping clean
The slate of the day
So that now, that which is past is past,
That which is possible is possible,
And tangled cobwebs of fear
Melt like snow under a summer's moon.
In the silence the darkness whispers,
"Leave judgments and assumptions behind;
See what is true
With your heart, not your eyes.
Abandon worries to moments gone by.
Sleep well,
And with the rising sun
Rise, too,
And write boldly, anew
On the clean slate of your life."

Evening 133.

As I lie down to rest
In the stillness of the night,
I consider the wonder of my heart.
Throughout the long day it serves me,
Without reminder, without instruction,
It performs a task most incredible.
Moment to moment,
Day to day,
The beautiful, powerful rhythm of life
Within the core of ourselves,
Intimate, precious,
The steady pulse of existence
Representing that which is patient,
Steadfast,
Faithful, and
Loving.
Time now to put aside work and worries,
To let peaceful thoughts enfold us and
Gentle shadows encircle us,
To sense the most wondrous
Beatings of our hearts
As they carry us
Lovingly,
Certainly
From moment to moment,
Into sleep,
Into dreams,
Into healing.

Evening 134.

Nightfall, a time familiar,
Profound, and
Beautiful.
Evening reaches across the heavens with
Silent, fire-red fingers,
Painting an ever-changing sky-scape
That amazes,
Quiets, calms.
Humankind, creations at once familiar
Profound and beautiful.
Eyes and hearts trained heavenward,
In awe, in wonder
Of space,
Time,
Existence.
Red shifts - indigo to steel to black.
Calmed and quieted by the darkness,
We train our eyes and hearts away from the sky
Toward each other,
In awe, in gratitude
For the loving souls who
Travel through
Space,
Time,
And existence with us.
Good night, friend.
Breathe easily.
Rest peacefully.
Sleep well.

Evening 135.

As the Earth turns to night again
And the chattering sounds of the world soften
Beneath a gentle blanket of darkness,
Calm the orchestra within your own mind;
Ease the frantic,
Sometimes tangled harmonies
That demand to be heard
Even when it is time to rest.
Let them fade away,
And seek, rather, that simple tune,
That peaceful, sweet melody at the core of your heart.
It is there, waiting,
Asking nothing but to soothe you,
To sing you into the quiet arms of the evening and
Into a healing sleep.

Evening 136.

Evening moves across the land, melting light and color, opening the sky to the stars and enfolding us within quiet darkness. In this precious, private time, let us turn our thoughts from the external to the internal. Let us free the fears and uncertainties that loomed large in the light of day. Let us find the seed of forgiveness for each other and for ourselves. Let us realize the humanity we embody and the love we possess. Let us become reacquainted with the powerful good that lives in our souls. And with this profound yet simple remembrance, let us rest. Let us sleep peacefully throughout the gentle night, knowing that as morning comes again, we will rise recovered, rested, and ready. Good night, friends.

Evening 137.

Draw the cover of night about your shoulders,
And lie down;
Close your eyes and let the weight of the day fall away.
Patient shadows will enfold you;
The gentle voice of darkness will whisper you
To your rest,
To sleep.
Then drift with leaves on an evening breeze,
Smile with the moon and
Rise up to the glorious, velvet-black sky.
Join the stars in their brilliant chorus
Of acceptance,
Of joy,
Of peace.
Good night.
Good night.

Evening 138.

Worried mind, let your fears fade with the dimming of day's light. Troubled heart, feel the gentle darkness as it surrounds you to comfort you. Wounded spirit, release your pain and doubts to the evening, for it is a time of healing, rest, and renewal. Beautiful soul, accept the powerful gifts of the night. They are meant for you. They wait for you. Sleep well, friend.

Evening 139.

Look out;
What do you see?
Bright daylight's wave withdrawing,
Soft darkness approaching,
A steady tide of time,
The night enfolding the land in gentle arms,
Offering the sanctuary of rest.
Look up;
What do you see?
The silent, sentinel moon,
Silver stars and golden galaxies spattered across
The vast and beautiful black canvas of sky,
A tapestry of wonder
Gloriously beyond perfect comprehension
And wondrously so.
Look within;
What do you see?
A mind filled with worries and wonders,
A heart seeking to love, struggling with fear,
A spirit striving, learning, hoping, growing,
With the tide of life,
A soul as important to the world
As every other soul,
As valuable and necessary to
What is, to what has been, and to what will be
As any now, then, or to come.
Do you see this?
Look;
It is there.
And now, with this comforting certainty,
Sleep.
Sleep well.
Good night.

Evening 140.

No need to resist the darkness,
The change from day to evening,
The rearrangements and dimming of light,
The scattering of reflections,
Impressions, expectations.
No need to cling to what was before,
To hesitate to reach out
Beyond what you can see,
For what lies in the stillness is a key to tomorrow,
What waits in these, the shadows of slumber,
Holds answers and insights,
Courage, strength, and recovery.
No need to fear the night,
It is what it is meant to be,
Whole and right.
And beneath fears and hesitations,
Deep in the stillness of your spirit,
You what you are meant to be,
Whole and right.
Breathe deeply and know this.
Feel your heartbeat and embrace this.
Then sleep well, friend.
Sleep well.

Evening 141.

The thoughtful night waits for you, holds out its hand, and
beckons you to rest. Surrender to its gentle whisper and
soothing embrace. Close your eyes against the turbulent
shadows of the past and uncertainties of the future. See,
rather, this very moment and know the completeness therein.
Feel the stillness and perfection. Know the peace, the release.
And then sleep. Sleep, my friend. Good night.

Evening 142.

Planets and stars,
Moon and misted galaxies;
Each night the Universe draws open its curtains,
Offering a show so profound that our minds cannot grasp the fullness.
And by this beautiful failing we are filled with wonder and awe,
Gratitude and humility,
And the glorious assurance of our place in it all.

Evening 143.

The night has come, offering quiet,
Offering serenity,
And yet our minds want to forge on,
Forge ahead,
Through the fading light and rising shadows,
Turning our burdens over and around to look at them
Again and again,
Struggling,
Tangled and exhausted,
Headlights seeking answers
Without direction.
But the spirit says,
Slow now,
Release it all,
Be still,
Be silent.
Your journey is for tomorrow.
Now, in the blessed darkness,
Hear your gentle heartbeats
Feel your peaceful breaths,
Relinquish your troubles, and
Sleep in evening's healing embrace.

Evening 144.

Candles of the night-sky,
Brilliant point within perfect blackness,
Keeping watch.
Profound, distant,
Existing as they are meant to,
Then, now, and into the unfathomable reach.
Stretching beyond, out
Across the silent vastness
To touch the candles of the night-land
That shine within the human soul.
Profound, steadfast,
Existing as they are meant to,
Then, now, and into the unfathomable reach;
Inextinguishable.
Glowing with hope,
Compassion, power and
Grace,
Keeping watch even as the body sleeps;
As perfect as a star,
As fearless as the Universe.
Sleep well, dear soul.
Good night.

Evening 145.

Drifting in darkness, together,
The night as familiar as our own heartbeats and
As gentle as a creator's touch;
We are at home in evening's great shadows,
In this perfect moment.
The moon sings softly in harmony
With the stars
And with all above,
Around
And beneath us.
Be comforted,
Rest well, friends,
And let fears fall behind you like
Old leaves on a midnight wind.
Sleep well, deeply, wholly,
And awaken to a new moment filled with
Perfect possibilities.

Evening 146.

As night moves in around you, offering its shawl of stillness and quiet, think back on the day. On the smile you received or gave, the encouraging words accepted or offered, the kindness extended or taken. Remember that which was thoughtful and loving, and throw away that which was hurtful. For the good rises up and overcomes the bad; mercy holds the power to heal the spirit-wounded. Freed, now, embrace the gentle and the merciful as a comforting blanket. Gather kindness to your heart, close your weary eyes, and sleep. Sleep well. Good night, friend.

Evening 147.

Quiet evening, speak softly. Let your gentle darkness enfold us, draw us close, ease our hearts, and bring us rest. Let us find peace. Let us sleep. Good night.

Evening 148.

Time of quiet,
Of calm,
Of stillness;
The world slows and settles once more into darkness,
Calling us to rest.
What, then, of our thoughts, when
Peace enfolds the land,
When the moon looks kindly down upon the earth and
Stars, glistening bits of heaven-dust, hold as they were
Tossed across the
Black canvas of eternity?
What of our thoughts
After the day,
Before the day,
In this, the now?
Let them be of gratitude.
Let them be of thankfulness.
Recall the compassionate and the courageous,
The generous and the tender,
The patient and the kind,
The gifts that surround you in all their
Forms both grand and modest.
And in this acknowledgement
Let the profound and surprising power of humbleness
Fill your soul,
Wash away worries and free you from fear.
Breathe in the beauty of this moment,
Of this night,
And know you are part of it all
Through the awesome gift of that which is.
Sleep well, friend.
Sleep well.

Evening 149.

The world is calm, dark;
The tide is low, the moon high,
And our hearts find rest.

Evening 150.

Darkness is not without substance,
Nor is it empty;
Night is not a hollow space between daylights,
But a time of true and certain purpose.
A time for minds to quiet,
For hearts to ease and gentle hopes to rise,
For souls to sing, stars to blaze, and
Fears to fade.
For hearts to beat and tenuous dreams to dare be dreamed.
To put aside burdens and set free regrets,
For hands to toss aside doubts and
Take hold the healing peace that awaits
In the darkness,
In the night,
In the blessed quiet beneath the stars.

Evening 151.

Dear friend, open your heart to the peace that comes as light recedes and shadows cover the earth once more. Surrender to the healing power of the gentle night. Shh, now. Be still. And in this tranquil moment, think back on the day gone by, and what was good. Think, then, on the day yet to come, and what you can make good. For in your hand you hold the quiet, the peace, the power. It is yours to keep and yours to share. Knowing this, sleep, my friend. Sleep well.

Evening 152.

Burdens of the day weigh
Heavily on heart and mind;
Things done or said,
Things yet to do or say,
Mistakes, misunderstandings,
Barriers,
Uncertainties.
But here, now, is the night,
The great and glorious time of silvered stars and
Fathomless space;
Eternity opened to fill
Our eyes with wonder
And our souls with peace.
Stop now;
Surrender to the
Quiet wisdom of the shadows.
Un-shoulder your troubles,
Put down your worries.
Give yourself the gifts of patience and understanding
You would ask of others.
Then draw close the blanket of assurance and comfort,
And sleep.
Sleep.
Good night.

Evening 153.

The night is here,
A dark and gentle blanket of peace and stillness;
A time for contemplation,
For letting go,
For rest.
Breathe out what was,
Breathe in the beauty of the now
And sleep.
Sleep well through the darkness and
Into morning,
Into the new day,
Into all things fresh
And possible.

Evening 154.

The night, with dignity both silent and grand,
Draws back the veil of light to reveal
The glorious and
Vast wonder of eternity.
The black Universe, embedded with countless stars,
Is opened that we might see;
That we might sense the profoundness of creation.
The evening, with quiet calm and authority,
Opens its hands to show that
There is nothing to hide,
Nothing to fear.
And then realize the truth;
You are in your rightful place,
Determined and certain,
Within the Great Mystery and Glory that is
Everything.
In knowing this, now, be humbled.
Humbled, find peace.
In peace, find rest.
In rest, find sleep.
In sleep, find healing and renewal.
Good night, friend.
Sleep well.

Evening 155.

Weariness is not weakness
Nor frailty,
But a reminder that
We are meant to surrender,
To rest,
To recover,
To renew.
The dark night is not frail
But powerful and purposeful,
An offering to all that breathe and move
Upon the earth,
A time that draws us near, folds around us,
And holds us close.
Weary soul, welcome the night.
Gentle night, comfort those who rest.
Let this partnership be as it is meant to be,
And sleep a most peaceful sleep, friend.

Evening 156.

Voice of the night,
Sing a song as soft as the light of distant stars,
As kind as the face of the smiling, silver moon,
As calm as the breathe of a resting world.
Voice of the night,
Speak in a whisper as peaceful as the hearts of the merciful,
As gentle as a loved one's touch,
As certain as a Divine benediction.
Voice of the night,
Remind me that in this moment all is well.
Remind me that I am not alone beneath the distant stars or
The silver moon.
Tell me, again, that I am part of this resting world
And that the benediction is mine.

Evening 157.

In this dark and silent night,
As our spirits turn and twist, restless
With the residuals of the day,
Let go and accept the peace of the evening,
For it is here.
Seek the gentleness, for it awaits.
Reach for the quiet calm,
The merciful understanding,
For they are here in these late hours,
Gifts to be touched, known, embraced.
Be assure that darkness is as kind as light;
Evening as right and good as morning.
Inhaling, exhaling,
Tides in, tides out,
Flower to seed to flower,
Each right in its own time.
And now, as the moon rises
And the stars awaken,
Seek rest, seek healing.
It is here,
It awaits,
Ready to be touched, known,
Embraced.
Sleep well, friend.
Good night.

Evening 158.

In time with the enduring rhythm of life and reality, the Universe, each night, reveals itself to the waiting eye and hopeful heart. In silent dignity, it draws back the day's bright veil, offering a star-strewn vista that is at once profound, startling, and gloriously familiar. The night reaches out, down, and surrounds us in its immeasurable and comforting embrace. It whispers in a voice known by the soul, reminding us of our connection to all below, beside, and above. "Look, see, and know. This is your home, both the solid ground beneath your feet and the eternal space beyond. Do not be distressed, for you are where you should be. Let go your fears. Breathe in peace. Find courage and compassion, and know that you are strong." We are not meant to respond, for words will fail. But, instead, we are meant to look and wonder, to see and remember, to release, to accept, to know. And then, as peace takes its rightful place within us, we are to sleep. And sleeping, we are to recover and renew, so when the day's bright sun rises once more, we will be ready, courageous, and compassionate toward one another. We will shine as stars upon the Earth. We will be strong.

Evening 159.

The sun has stepped back and away
With silent dignity,
Taking the day with it,
Beckoning the night to take its rightful place
Over the land,
Over us.
Let the darkness be a comfort,
A time of solace and
Peace.
Put down your worries and burdens.
Do not fret over them,
Nor struggle with them;
Those that need tending will wait until the
Day returns
And you are healed.
Those which are but residual uncertainties,
Fears without substance,
Will drift and fade and be gone
As mist in a bright morning.
Open your spirit, then, to the night's comfort;
Surrender to the solace and the peace,
And sleep well, friend.
Sleep well.

Evening 160.

May this night bring you peace of mind and a quietness of spirit. May your heart be comforted, knowing that what came before is gone and what is to come is still unformed. This, then, is your moment; it has opened its arms to you, offering its gift of rest. Accept the gift. Allow yourself the blessing of serenity, the benediction of the silvered darkness and of golden stars, of gentle breezes and of silent wonder. Sleep well, friend. Good night.

Evening 161.

Echoes of the day reverberate into the night,
Waves, rippling from light into darkness;
Fearful ones kept in motion by wearied focus,
Turned over and over again in tired minds.
Joyous ones kept alive in the beat of a grateful heart,
Flowing gently with each easing breath.
Let the turbulent echoes quiet,
And the troubled waves go still.
Let the joyful echoes reassure you that all is well;
Let them enfold you, comfort you,
And sing you to a healing sleep.

Evening 162.

The day is finished,
The melody of its verse written
And engraved on the soul of memory;
The joys, the struggles, the blessings.
Night is here now
To compose the interlude,
The peaceful bridge that will carry us
Through the gentle darkness;
A lullaby that knows well
The symphony of our lives
As it is written day by day,
And reaches from one to the other
To create a soft bed of dreams
In tune with the evening sky.
Rest now, as the stars sing
To the measure of your breaths
And the rhythm of your heartbeat.
Sleep well.
Good night.

Evening 163.

As night arrives, bearing gifts of darkness,
Quietness, and countless, brilliant, smiling stars;
As the Universe opens to reveal the vastness of eternity
And wonder of creation,
May our hearts and minds open, also,
To welcome thoughts of forgiveness.
May we let go that which may have hurt or offended us,
Shaking off the weight of resentment,
And setting it free to blow away
On an evening breeze.
Forgiveness of others;
Forgiveness of ourselves.
As the world gives up day for night,
And one moment gives itself up for the next,
Let us give up anger for understanding
And find the peace and wonder that take its place.
Then, relieved and unburdened,
May we sleep deeply
And sleep well.
Good night.

Evening 164.

On a beautiful night, with the day behind and the stars overhead, we feel ourselves one with nature, with God, with the most beautiful and grand All.

Evening 165.

Comes the darkness,
The cool, the stillness;
The star-dusted night
Enfolds the Earth,
As familiar as a friend,
As profound as its Divine directive,
Wholly grand and unfathomable,
Wholly close and comforting.
Ponder if you so desire,
Imagine and wonder and question
How is it, that it is.
Or contemplate nothing
But rather let go,
Breathe deeply of the kind, glorious evening
And let your soul spiral
Around,
Up,
And into gentle dreams.

Evening 166.

The night sky,
Dark, deep, and endless,
Dotted with patterns, points of silver,
And dusted with distant worlds,
May, at times, be crossed by clouds,
Threaded filaments or heavy battings
That obscure the vast, beautiful blackness,
That draw a veil between ourselves and the
Grand Vision.
Such are fears and doubts,
Creating barriers that limit our sights,
Forcing our thoughts inward to
Tumble over each other,
Causing our eyes to cast downward.
Weary, we cannot fathom that which exists
On the other side of the veil.
Exhausted, we no longer look up.
Yet clouds are fragile and temporary;
The Universe remains glorious and
Unchanged by fleeting shrouds.
Fears, too, ride the whim of the wind,
And doubts break apart when we lift our gazes
To discover the greater reality that lies beyond the haze.
This night, let your fears fade and your doubts melt,
Know that you are stronger than your troubles,
And the Truth of what is Good
Is greater by far than that
Which would keep you from seeing it.
Then sleep well, friend.
Sleep well.

Evening 167.

Feel the night, the stillness, the darkness, the great peace beyond and the great peace within. Breathe it, surrender to it, know the freedom that comes with being part of everything that is. Then sleep, friend. Good night.

Evening 168.

Overcome
By burdens,
Uncertainties,
Tasks undone and
Un-begun,
Head down,
Eyes close,
Drained,
Wearied.
Now comes the evening,
Still,
Quite,
With whispered assurances
That strength will return in time,
And clarity,
And certainty.
The night holds out its gift of rest
Asking nothing in return.
Sense the power of the
Gentle darkness as it surrounds you;
Be overcome
With peace.

Evening 169.

I am the night,
The rising moon,
The falling stars, the dark tree shadows;
I am the air,
Filled up with songs,
Of night-borne birds and firefly meadows.
I gently fall upon the mountains,
I reach across the sea and plain,
I hold at bay the bright day's morning,
Until the world has turned again.
I am the night,
No pride, no boasting,
But only what I'm meant to be;
You are of worth,
In equal measure,
Dear child of Earth,
Sleep well, good night.

Evening 170.

May the breath of the night wind, the rhythm of the tides, the gentleness of the dark earth, and the heartbeat of the vast, star-filled sky bring you comfort, peace of mind, and a deep, healing sleep. Good night, friend.

Evening 171.

Hands that work,
Put aside your tasks.
Minds that struggle,
Step back from the battle.
Hearts that ache,
Release the pain
Into the silence that surrounds you.
For now, surrender to the night.
For now, let peace embrace you and hold you.
For now, sleep.
Rest, dear one.
It will be better.
It will be well.

Evening 172.

The darkness of night
Is not enemy of the light.
It is simply what it is meant to be,
A time of tranquility and stillness,
An offering to a world that often
Seems to spin too hard,
Too fast,
To a life that sometimes races
Our heartbeats as if there was something
Un-winable to be won.
The evening is a gentle time to be,
To reflect,
To heal,
To prepare for morning;
It offers the gift of comfort that we,
Upon awakening,
May carry into our bright, new day.
Breathe in the quiet, then;
Find the peace you are meant to find.
Sleep well.
Good night.

Evening 173.

The vast, glorious night,
Reaching out with star-dusted fingers,
Offers a blanket of darkness,
Of softness,
Of dreams and floating
Wonders,
Of gentle stillness,
And rest.
Surrender, now.
Be enfolded,
Be comforted,
Be carried away into the softness,
The darkness,
The dreams and wonders,
That await to bring peace
And renewal.
Sleep well, friend.
Good night.

Evening 174.

Can we fathom a field,
The workings of each and every flower at any given moment,
As buds opens and leaves turn their faces toward the light
And the wind stirs them into frantic, joyous dance?
Or can we comprehend the whole of the sea in one thought,
Every creature that dwells there,
Rising upon swells that flash in the sun,
Diving to dark depths
On silvery fin?
Can we grasp the entirety of the vast night's sky that reveals
itself
Above us as day withdraws?
Can we know the whole of each star, each galaxy that splashes
The black canvas with its crystalline paint?
The swirling matter and spinning planets
And reflective moons that ride the
Currents of their benign masters?
Can we hold in one thought the totality of
The Universe?
Of distance and time
And timelessness?
Such is wonder,
Such is awe.
Such is the startling breath of astonishment
And the cleansing rush of humbleness that
Is right and good,
Allowing us to let go of small worries and frets,
To surrender to the grandness of existence,
In surrendering,

Finding our rightful place,
In finding our place,
Finding peace.
And in finding peace,
Sleeping well.
In sleeping well,
Gaining renewed strength to
Turn our faces
Toward the light as day returns,
To open our hearts,
To dive and rise and dance
As we are meant to dance.

Evening 175.

Rest easily, friend;
Night has spread her soft blanket
With you in her thoughts.

Evening 176.

Apprehensions, like frantic insects,
Stir the night air,
Alighting, buzzing, spinning worthless circles
That the wearied mind's eye seems fated to follow,
Round and round,
Creating a fatigue that resists rest.
Turn away from them;
Look away.
Find, instead, that bright spot within your soul,
The memory of something lovely and compassionate,
The knowledge of something kind and true.
And the power of its goodness will
Hold your mind, calm your thoughts,
And bring you
A peaceful sleep.
Good night, friend.
Good night.

Evening 177.

Creatures of the evening sing in the darkness beyond the window screens. Peaceful sounds that untangle the day and create a comforting bed for all of creation. Sleep well.

Evening 178.

No need to grasp on to the day,
To fear its release, its disappearance,
For it is meant to drift away;
Another will take its place,
Tomorrow.
For now, sunlight fades and vanishes,
Starlight takes its place.
Moments move into moments;
We travel with them
And with the earth and the wind and the dark and shifting
skies,
Drifting with the night
And into gentle sleep,
Watched over by stars,
Held in the heart of the heavens.

Evening 179.

Darkness arrives and sunlight fades away,
Shadows link hands and on the land they lay,
Waves on the sea reflect the moon's soft glow,
Stars high above smile at the world below.
Time now has come to put our tasks aside,
That which is still, a kindly, peaceful guide,
Follow the path of quiet and of calm,
Night will enfold us with its healing balm.
Lie down as evening's winds pass gently by,
Sleep, safe and blessed, beneath the endless sky.

Evening 180.

Breath of night, breathe kindly,
Gently upon us;
Wings of night, carry us tenderly,
For we are weary and in need of sleep;
Voice of night, speak softy,
And remind us that
In spite of the darkness,
The stillness,
The silence,
We are not alone,
Never forgotten,
That there is strength to recover,
And peace to be found,
As we rest and heal
In the Heart of God.

Evening 181.

Darkness hides only that which is seen by the eyes, while those things that are seen by the soul need no light. Love lives on throughout the brilliant day and across the reach of the deepest night, unfazed, unfettered. The sun will rise and set, the stars will shine then retreat. Life will begin and end. But love that we give freely will always be remembered; and love we receive will be with us into eternity.

Evening 182.

Alone
In the night;
Shadows at our feet,
Clinging to the trees, the hillsides,
Veiling all that is familiar
In darkness.
Sadness weighs heavy;
Weariness clings to hearts,
Distancing us from what is there,
Making us feel even more
Alone.
But stop.
Look up.
There are stars in the sky,
And a silvered moon,
Glowing eternally and joyously,
Singing in wordless song,
"You do not need to see to know
That you are not alone.
Darkness is not haughty, but kind.
Reach out, then, and do not cower.
Friends are there, and love,
And comfort,
And peace.
Surrender to this moment,
And rest."

Evening 183.

Farewell, fair day,
Greetings, gentle night.
As you are meant to be
Be calm and still,
Powerful, serene.
As you are created to do
Offer rest and relief,
Recovery, healing.
In your vast, deep shadows
We will put down our burdens,
Un-shoulder our troubles,
And release our fears
To blow away on a dark, thoughtful breeze.
We will embrace this quiet moment
And will be the peace we seek.
Good night, night.
Now we sleep.
Good night.

Evening 184.

May the quiet of the night silence your worries. May the stillness of the night calm your fears. May the gentle embrace of the night comfort you, ease your heart, and bring you the rest you so rightly deserve. Surrender to the sacred darkness and sleep well. Beautiful dreams to you.

Evening 185.

Lights low, star-glow,
Winds blow, hearts know –
Day is done,
Let go.

Evening 186.

Even when the moon and the stars are hidden from sight,
Shrouded in mist or cloud,
They are indeed overhead, steadfast, certain,
Writing upon the Universe
A verse that speaks your name,
A song sung just for you.

Evening 187.

Shrug off the weight of the day;
Put it aside.
What must be taken care of
Will wait until morning,
While unfounded, fearful residues
Will drift away on an evening breeze.
Inhale peace.
Exhale regrets.
Allow yourself the gentle kindness
You would offer a beloved friend,
Then surrender to the quiet darkness.
Sleep deeply.
Sleep well. friend.
Good night.

Evening 188.

The evening hangs weightless,
Above, around, beneath;
Gentle shadows reach out to surround us all,
Leaving no space unaffected,
No living thing untouched.
For all land is sacred and deserving of peace,
And every soul of value and meriting rest.

Evening 189.

The sun has retreated
And the moon has danced in to take her place.
Silvery stars spatter the vast black canopy overhead
While below, leaves spin in a midnight dance
Through field and forest.
Nocturnal creatures arise from their slumber
To prowl,
To fly,
With agate eye and wing.
Yet this dark and quiet moment
Is our time to rest.
Let us surrender to the warm,
Gentle touch of weariness.
Let us accept the kind, insistent whispers of the night,
Reminding us to let go and
To sleep.
To dream.
To heal.
To find peace beneath the moon and the silvery stars
As foxes roam
And owls soar through field and forest.
Good night, friend.
Good night.

Evening 190.

As the sun sets and darkness rolls silently in, become like the night. Quiet, still, and calm. Do not worry about what was or will be, but accept the moment that is. Fell the warmth of sleepiness surround you; know the peace that is offered from the evening's gentle hand. And rest well, friend.

Evening 191.

Claim the night,
Child of Earth.
Breathe of the sweet evening air,
Listen intently to the dark winds
And the certain beatings of your heart.
Consider the stars that hold their assigned places
In the everlasting sky,
And the moon in its charming phase,
So quiet,
Content.
Claim the night;
Let worries fall away
And gentle peace move in.
You are as worthy as the air, the winds,
The stars, sky,
And moon.
No fear can reduce you,
No burden incomplete can diminish you.
Know this truth and
Claim the night,
Child of Earth.
Then rest,
Rejoice,
And fly free in your dreams.
Sleep well, friend.
Sleep well.

Evening 192.

Silence and darkness
Have come; hear your soul whisper,
"Shh, dear friend, sleep. Sleep."

Evening 193.

Night is here;
A time of darkness,
Quiet, and
Peace.
As we lie down and pull
The soft cover of sleep around our shoulders,
May our thoughts turn away from
Those of dissatisfaction and
Toward those of gratitude.
For both dissatisfaction and gratitude,
Given the space of night, will grow.
How much more lovely,
How much more worthwhile
To nurture the flowers
Of thankfulness
Than the thorns of regret.
Let appreciation for all we are,
All we've experienced
And all that lies ahead
Rise up around us.
Let it drift to the moon and stars
And carry our joyous souls with it
Into perfect rest and healing.

Evening 194.

Weep, if you must, into the arms of the night,
Into the darkness
And deep, quiet shadows.
For the night is a time for letting go,
For coming to,
For recovering.
Sing, if you will, and join the chorus of
Jubilant stars;
Listen to the joyful song of the wind,
For the night is a time to celebrate
And acknowledge the wonders that surround you
And are you.
Pray, if you might, beneath the vast and glorious
Sky where a moment and eternity
Come together, merging
Into what is and will always be;
For the night is a time to
Exhale in gratitude
And be awed by the grandeur
Of creation and its Creator
As your heart and soul have come to understand them.
Sleep, if you shall, in the peace of silence
And the beauty of stillness,
For the night is a gift,
Offered unconditionally,
Generously,
Without expectation.
It is ours.
It is yours.
Rest well, then.
Good night.

Evening 195.

Tonight, be as gentle with yourself as the darkness is gentle with the Earth, as kind as golden moonlight is to the forests and hills; as easy and soft as crystalline star-glow is upon the rhythmic waves of the sea. Let go your regrets and un-shoulder your burdens. Step away then turn back to see yourself as you would a beloved friend; then offer a sympathetic shoulder and understanding heart. The evening is the time to release, recover, renew, and then surrender to perfect rest beneath the watchful moon and the vigilant stars. Sleep deeply, friend. Sleep well until morning comes 'round again.

Evening 196.

This day is past and the
New one not yet born.
Here, in night's dark and
Gentle moment,
Open your hands
And mind
To release that which
Binds you to the past and the future.
It is now that you are to be;
It is now that sleep offers to encircle you,
Hold you,
And bring you peace.
Rest well, friend.

Evening 197.

As the night's gentle arms surround us, we find ourselves alone with ourselves. And in that time, in those hours of blessed darkness, we are able to throw off the frustrations of the day, set our hearts and minds free, and then drift to into a healing sleep.

Evening 198.

Sky-lamp moon, pin-hole stars,
Give glimpses into eternity
By way of the black vastness of the night's sky,
The silent, unfathomable Universe.
We shall never grasp it all;
It is meant for us to wander and wonder,
To question, to ponder.
Yet we shall know enough in this peaceful moment,
For the darkness whispers gentle revelations to the heart,
Assuring us that this is the time to rest,
To become one with the night and to sleep.
To dream.
To be healed.
Good night, friend.
Sleep well.

Evening 199.

Night sounds –
Distant trains and owls,
Rustling winds,
Clocks,
Footsteps and breaths,
Heartbeats;
Morph within the darkness,
Meld,
Braid into a single sound,
A voice that sings to us in whispered song.
Hear it.
Listen.
Then put down your worries,
Open your soul and set free your fears.
Let peace settle like moon dust upon your shoulders,
And the certainty of your worth rest gently upon your brow.
May sleep enfold and hold you until
Morning.

Evening 200.

Cat's purr, puppy's snores,
Close and cozy, soft, still,
Nighttime's blanket; sleep.

Evening 201.

Weariness is not an affliction
Or a weakness,
But rather a gift of the night,
Given to the body
To renew the mind
And heal the spirit.
Surrender to the sweetness of sleep.
Give in to the peaceful caress of
Silvery moonlight
And find rest beneath the
Silent, watchful eye of the glorious, star-strewn sky.
Good night, friend.
Good night.

Evening 202.

By day's end your shoulders may be bowed
Beneath pains or regrets,
Fears or sadness.
Life's struggles and cares
Weigh heavily,
Burdens that, when energy is spent,
Seem beyond hope
Or resolution.
Yet the night is here,
Still and peaceful,
Calm and powerful,
Offering a time of
Quiet relief and healing.
For strength renews in rest,
And clarity in sleep.
Allow yourself what is offered;
Let the gentle voice of the evening
Soothe the uncertainty in your soul
And remind you that you are not alone.
Let that which is grand,
That which is is Divine
Take and hold what must be held
And blow away that which should be discarded.
Then rest, friend.
Sleep deeply and well.

Evening 203.

Sing the song of the Universe! The tune you know in your heart, the melody that swells joyously in your spirit. Recall it, think on it, and let it play in your soul. It is as much a part of you as your breath, and you as much a part of it as the Earth and the stars. Sing the song of the Universe! No need for words tonight, only the music and the power it shares.

Evening 204.

Evening has arrived,
And with it a deep and peaceful darkness,
Its gift to Earth.
As blazing stars and galaxies keep watch from the eternal sky,
Let rest heal your heart and quiet your mind.
Let sleep silence worries, doubts.
Accept this truth as you drift into the night, and be comforted.
Your course is not set;
Each moment offers countless possibilities
For change, for new directions,
New trajectories, understandings, perceptions.
You are no more static than the blazing stars and whirling galaxies
In the immeasurable Universe;
And as those jewels of the night withdraw,
Giving way again for the morning's sun,
Rise up to set your new path,
Embrace your new directions,
Restored, strengthened,
And joyous once more.

Evening 205.

Gentle, darkest night,
Spreads its soft blanket for us;
Peace, then, friend. Sleep well.

Evening 206.

Though the night is dark and still,
And sometimes we feel alone
Within its silence,
Let us leave our heart-lights on for one another,
Kind and gentle thoughts
That, like bright stars, radiate
Certainty amid the uncertainty,
And offer steady beacons of comfort.
Let these lights ease our minds and
Guide us, safely, home
To our souls.
To ourselves.
Sleep well, friend.
Good night.

Evening 207.

A day has ended,
A moment, a scene,
A chapter of life,
A page turned.
Finished yet unfinished,
Poured out, wrung out, spent;
Night calls you to sleep,
To let go and embrace the interlude
Provided by sweet darkness
And gentle silence.
Your story will wait;
The book of your life remains open.
So rest now, and well,
And when morning returns you shall
Begin again to write your story
As you hope it to be,
As you dream it to be,
As you strive for it to be.

Evening 208.

And now in this evening's hour, amid the silent shadows and faint moonlight, let time stand still. Do not think of the past nor the future. Be outside of time, and there, surrounded by all that is eternal, be know peace.

Evening 209.

Rain on a window glass distorts only our vision, not that which lies beyond the pane. Darkness hides the world from view but does not send it away. You are not less than anything that exists, even when hopes and courage wane. That which is, is. That which is true, is true. And therefore, as day has withdrawn and night has arrived, know that nothing good will be lost in the evening's stillness and silence; know that within this grand Creation you are not alone. Do not fret with sad imaginings, but release your fears and accept the healing sleep that is offered. Good night, then, friend. Rest well.

Evening 210.

How easily wounded, left raw, burned;
Rattled and hurt we can become.
A universal experience;
Every spirit at some point, on some day,
In some moment,
Worn down, defeated,
Tears shed or fought back,
Pained.
Yet without fail the day fades away and night arises,
Casting, bathing the sky in
Scarlet, brilliant,
Azure-ash,
Silent Black;
Spreading great, benevolent wings over all,
Quiet shelter for the saddened heart
And rest to the exhausted body.
Now is time to release the pain,
Let go the hurt,
Receive the comfort and
Tender consolation.
Forgive.
Breathe deeply of the evening air;
Wounds will heal,
Tears will cease,
And sleep will enfold you,
Strengthen you,
And carry you through the gentle darkness
Into the kindness of a bright new morning.

Evening 211.

Gratitude
For the day,
The rising, sustained light,
And all it offers –
Awareness, opportunities,
Moments to act, to learn;
Moments to be.
Gratitude
For others,
Friends and family,
Foes and those we've not yet met,
And all they offer to our lives, our insights, our growth.
Gratitude
For ourselves,
The potentials we've discovered and will discover,
The kindnesses we've shared.
Gratitude
For the night,
The rising, all-encompassing darkness
And all it offers –
Stillness, sleep,
Moments to recover strength and clarity;
Moments to be.

Evening 212.

With a steady hand, Night slowly, steadily reveals the brilliantly dark and eternal vastness of creation. Look up and look out. Breathe it in; take it in. Know that you are no more and no less than the galaxies, the moons, and the very Earth beneath our feet. And with that humbling, affirming certainty, open your mind and release your fears and resentments. Open your heart and let the peace of the moment settle upon you like gentle, healing stardust. Sleep well, then, friend. Good night.

Evening 213.

Darkness folds around us
And in the shadowed silence,
The stillness of the night,
We are gently reminded that we have enough.
Enough sunlight and starlight,
Enough time and space,
Enough within ourselves to find contentment,
To discover kindness,
Hope,
And creative goodness;
To be what we are and to encounter strengths that might yet
lie
Dormant inside.
Therefore release the knotted fear of want and inadequacy;
Unclench the fists that cling to
That which is imagined critical, yet is only
Burdensome.
Breathe deeply, slowly, of the sweet evening air that is now,
Then shake loose your worries,
Release your doubts to the wind,
And sleep well, friend.
Sleep well.

Evening 214.

In our minds, the patterns,
In our hearts, the fabrics, woven,
In our hands, the threads.
With these
We craft the quilts of our lives,
One piece at a time
One day at a time;
Some sections sewn hastily
Rushed,
With little thought,
A bit ragged, tattered.
Yet others fashioned carefully
With courage and compassion,
Lovely, strong, brilliant.
When day has ended and night has arrived,
May our lives' quilts
Be warm enough, strong enough, beautiful
And large enough
To enfold not only ourselves but those around us,
That we might sleep in the peace we have created
For one another
And have offered to each other.

Evening 215.

The night rolls in, quietly, steadily, covering the land in gentle darkness, offering rest to those who are weary. May your troubles be put aside and your mind be at ease; may sleep enfold you and hold you until morning returns. Good night, friend.

Evening 216.

Come the shadows on the land
As sunlight fades away,
Tender night will take its place
And keep your fears at bay.
Gone your worries, sorrows, doubts,
Burdens, left behind;
The evening offers rest and hope,
To ease your troubled mind.
Sleep now, friend, beneath the stars,
Below the kindly moon,
Feel the healing, comfort, joy,
Hear nighttime's gentle tune.

Evening 217.

Do not fear the night,
The vanishing of the light,
The cloaking of the world in shadow and silence.
Do not fret nor worry over that which that cannot be seen
Nor determined within the darkness.
For while we, weary and uncertain,
Might imagine that which is hidden is unpleasant,
It is as likely to be something glorious,
Beautiful,
Unexpected and welcomed,
Waiting to reveal itself as the sun
When it breaks through storm clouds,
Waiting to awaken your heart and soul
To new chances, fresh hopes.
Accept the night, then, patiently,
Gratefully,
And sleep.
Come the morning,
Arise and
Step into the newness of the day,
The newness of you.

Evening 218.

The night is never so long that day does not return,
And the darkness is never so deep that light is abolished.
Night and darkness are equals of day and light,
A beautiful balance of work and repose,
Wakefulness, slumber,
Holding, releasing,
Striving, surrendering.
Claim, then, the night as your own,
The darkness as a comfort.
Let its purpose serve its purpose;
Find rest in the gentle arms of evening,
And sleep well, my friend.
Be well through the darkness and into the rising light.
Good night.
Good night.

Evening 219.

Morning is for rising, daylight for working, evening for contemplating, and nighttime for healing. Yet all of them – morning, day, evening, and night – are for giving and receiving love.

Evening 220.

Welcome, Earth, the kindly night,
When sun-bright day has taken flight.
Lands awash in darkness, still,
With shadows heavy on the hill;
Pewter clouds and misted trees,
Moonlit rivers, star-lit seas.
Follow to the shore of rest
And find your spirit gently blessed.
Close your eyes and free your soul
To fly toward its blissful goal
Of healing, comfort, joy most deep,
That hold you as you fall asleep.

Evening 221.

The music of eternity plays out across the Universe,
In and from every star and planet,
Every moon and swirling body.
In and from every thing that lives
And does not live,
In and from every conscious spirit
And yearning heart.
We are part of the orchestra,
Music makers of our moment,
Our songs both sad and jubilant,
Robust and wearied.
Rising up, loud and clear,
And fading to near silence;
Rhythmic,
As steady as morning to afternoon to twilight.
And as day fades into evening,
And the swirling Universe
Is revealed above us yet again in the vast, dark sky,
We are offered an interlude,
A time to pause, to rest, to recover and prepare
For the next stanza,
The next chorus
Of our lives.
Surrender, then, and let the gentle music of eternity
Lull you to sleep,
And bring you peace.
Good night until we join the chorus again
Tomorrow.

Evening 222.

Nighttime is a slow dance
Between your soul and the Universe;
Floating, drifting,
Rising up beyond the silvered moon,
Free and unburdened.
Let the evening enfold you;
Follow its lead, turning 'round easily,
Moving among the
Gently smiling stars.
Feel the song of peace surrounding you,
Warm, familiar,
Settling in your heart
And singing you to sleep.

Evening 223.

Even in the night,
As darkness pools around us,
Nothing good is lost.

Evening 224.

When darkness comes and day has danced away,
Turn thoughts away from that which is beyond
And focus, instead, on that which is within;
Breathe with your spirit,
Press your hand against the heart of your soul and
Feel the goodness that resides there.
This is true and certain and familiar;
Hold it gently
And sleep.
When day has returned,
You will hold it still, and carry it with you;
A familiar and certain light that
Illuminates,
Comforts, and
Guides us.
Sleep well.

Evening 225.

For quiet and tranquility,
For scarlet sunsets blazed across the sky
And stars that lift the vast canopy of blackness overhead.
For the moon that pours its light and soul out
Freely upon the Earth,
And breezes that carry the calls of night birds past the
window.
For friends long past, those of now and yet to come,
For heartbeats and warm beds,
Tender memories and soft pillows,
For joys recalled and reverence of spirit,
For this moment and those that lie ahead
Let us be grateful.
And in our gratitude,
Let us accept the tender gift of sleep.
Good night, friend.
Good night.

Evening 226.

Diamond stars lie scattered in joyous abandon
Across the vast, velvet-blackness of eternity as
A smiling silver moon silently looks on.
With such gloriously divine artwork
Drifting
And shifting
Above us,
With the tender Earth breathing
And whispering
Gently beneath us,
Let us be comforted.
For this is our rightful place
Among it all,
A part of it all.
Let us surrender to the arms of sleep.
Let us know healing.
Let us know peace.
Good night.

Evening 227.

Without a sound the sun moves on,
Around, down, away;
The face of the turning Earth softens, dims.
Colors reach out for one another
In the fading light,
Shifting, coming together as one;
Vivid greens and reds and golds and blues to
Forest, burgundy, bittersweet, sapphire,
Navy,
Charcoal,
Black.
And now, in that quiet darkness, the colors rest,
To rise again come morning.
In that quiet darkness, let us come together
In heart,
Our spirits reaching out to one another
In kindness,
Forgiveness,
Goodwill.
Our minds comforted, quieted,
Our souls serene.
May we rest, then,
To rise again
Come morning.

Evening 228.

Day surrenders, sunlight flees,
Darkness, starlight, gentle breeze.
Shadows, perfect, silent, still,
Night-black trees upon the hill.
Rivers spangled by the moon,
Distant train sings lonely tune.
Waves roll 'neath the vast, grand sky,
Earth lets out a gentle sigh;
Wearied souls lie down to sleep,
Peaceful quiet, comfort deep.
Rest now, all within the night,
Love and kindness be your light.

Evening 229.

Shadows on the floor,
Nightlight glow, tick-ticking clock,
Surrender now; sleep.

Evening 230.

Moonbeam, at times, shine against clouds, not concerned with whether they reach the earth or not, but shining because they are meant to shine. You, too, are meant to shine. Do not be concerned that what you share becomes hindered. For as moonbeams will, in time, reach the night-darkened trees and brighten the shadowed fields, so will your good offerings reach their destinations and brighten shadowed hearts. Sure of this, then, sleep well. The moon is shining, and so are you.

Evening 231.

Golden moon laced by fragile-ribboned clouds,
Stars punctuate the eternal blackness
With countless silver smiles;
Night is here again.
Spirits rise up effortlessly within the silence,
Souls reach out, freely and peacefully,
To touch the smiling Source,
To rejoice and welcome
Rest and healing.
Night is here again.
Sleep well, friend.
Sleep well.

Evening 232.

Eyes close,
Breaths slow,
Spirits surrender.
Sweet whispers of the gentle darkness,
Caresses of evening breezes
And the tender certainty of night's comforting arms.
Let go, then,
Give in;
Free yourself to a healing sleep.
Good night, friend.
Peaceful dreams.

Evening 233.

Let evening and darkness come as they will,
Bringing nothing ill nor spiteful,
But only offerings of silence, stillness,
A soft, starlit bed to cradle us
And spirit-bright wings to
Lift us from Earth-bound burdens into
The rapturous, healing freedom of
All that is and
All that can be.
Surrender.
Be restored.
Good night, friend.
Good night.

Evening 234.

Move into the night, swept up by moonlight into the starlit beyond. There, heart and spirit are reminded of the vast eternal of which they are part. Free now, fear dissolves, melts. Fly on, renewed, relieved. Sleep well, sleep deeply. Peace through the darkness and into the time of the rising sun.

Evening 235.

Waves tangle the sands of the shore;
Winds tangle the grasses of the fields.
Troubles tangle the mind and heart,
Rushing back and forth,
Whirling thoughts into unsettled dust.
Yet within the rushing,
Amid the dust,
I am surprised to find
A gratitude for the tangles
And confusions.
They remind me that there is
Still much to learn in this life,
Much to consider,
Much to gain by opening the
Clenched fist of perception
And letting the waves and winds have their ways a while.
So now, as the world has
Released the day and welcomed the night,
I release the fear of uncertainty
And welcome the peace that comes with knowing
I don't know it all.
I will sleep in this gentle darkness;
I will rest,
And upon awakening,
May find new light shining on the waves,
Fresh air stirring the grasses,
And new readiness to learn what the day
Might offer.

Evening 236.

Evening arrives,
Darkness covers the land;
Time to let go of nagging worries,
To shrug off vexing doubts that cling, tangled and unwanted,
To the mind.
What is done and past
Is done and past.
Release them,
Be freed.
Come morning, new moments and new chances will present
themselves,
But until then
May peace cover your heart as a warm and comforting
blanket,
And bring you a deep, healing sleep.

Evening 237.

Bells of the night chime silently,
Calling us to rest;
Heard by the spirit,
Known by the soul.
Follow their lead into the gentle dance of sleep.

Evening 238.

The same moon circles us,
The same crystalline stars surround us,
The same misty galaxy nests us.
Together, on this tiny Earth within the vast and unfathomable
Universe,
We turn from the sun toward the beautiful darkness of night.
As much a part of this glorious and vast creation as the kindly
moon,
The blazing sun,
The misty galaxy and the distant stars,
Breathe out the troubles of the day,
Shake off the dust of doubt
And claim this time of peace.
Sleep well and sleep deeply.
Good night.

Evening 239.

Silently, inevitably,
The wave of darkness washes
Over hill,
Field,
Forest,
Lake,
Farm,
City.
Rising up as a gentle, velvet giant,
Bearing down with kindly hands;
The night spreads out its blanket for us
And we are moved to rest.
Sleep well, friend.
Good night.

Evening 240.

Kind and predictable moon
Steady even as it seems to change,
Ebbing, flowing, silver-lit,
Drifting on course,
Never strayed, never lost;
A watchful eye in the vast, black sky.
Distant, yet the fingers of our spirits
Can touch its softness
And the hearts of our souls
Know the caress of its mist-filtered glow.
Strong and certain Love,
Steady even as it seems to change,
With us,
Watchful,
Never strayed, never lost,
Touching us with its
Gentle, unconditional caress,
Embracing us with
Perfect understanding and forgiveness.
Be comforted, then,
And sleep in the benevolent arms of Love,
Beneath the watchful light of the moon.

Evening 241.

You have lived another day, have attempted something, have accomplished something. Now rest, and sleep well, friend.

Evening 242.

We see the sunset as we do,
Golden or crimson,
Muted or brilliant.
We hear the evening sounds as we do,
Faint or clear,
Melodic and rhythmic or ambient, calm.
We feel the coming darkness as we do,
Cool or warm,
Powerful and awesome or gentle, tender.
However you perceive the arrival of night,
However it enfolds and holds you,
May you find the comfort you seek,
The peace you long for,
And the healing rest that prepares you
For the rising of the sun
And the coming of the new day.

Evening 243.

Shadowed tree,
Silent moon,
Distant hill,
Resting bird,
Chirring insect,
Ripping lake,
Falling star,
Sleeping soul.
All have their stories,
Their nobleness,
Their worth.
Remember this as you put your head to pillow;
No matter what the day held for you,
No matter what your doubts or regrets,
You are no less than the tree, the moon, the hill,
The bird, the insect, the lake or star.
Part of your story has been written
And lies behind you;
A new one awaits.
Sleep well, now, and sleep deeply,
And renewed and healed by the gift of rest
You will rise in the morning,
To begin a bright new chapter filled with clarity,
Possibilities,
Hope.

Evening 244.

Twilight's gentle shadows pooling, gathering,
Heralding night's arrival
In robes of satin blackness and
A crown of silver stars.
Benevolent hour, calling to bed beast and bird,
Field and forest.
The time has come to put down your burdens and
Lift up your heart;
Welcome the rest that evening holds out
Generously, gently.
May it surround and comfort you.
May it bring you peace.
Sleep well.
Sleep well.

Evening 245.

Delightful darkness
Whispers as our closest friend,
"I love you. Good night."

Evening 246.

Golden moon, soft, constant,
Face of peace in the evening sky.
Watchful, quiet,
Traveling slowly, steadily onward through the night
Into morning.
Even in the darkness reflecting warmth and kindness
Over town and city,
Forest, mountain,
Lake, river,
And the vast and glorious sea;
Reminding us to reflect warmth and kindness
As we travel forward through the night and into the
Coming morning,
Into the bright new day.

Evening 247.

Breathe in the night, the cool, the quiet,
Inhaling and accepting,
Exhaling and surrendering,
Becoming aware in the calm of the darkness
That all that breathe and live share the night, as well;
The cool, the quiet,
The air.
Let this remembrance of our connectedness be a comfort.
Let us be assured that we are never alone,
And that nothing can cast us out
Or make us less than we are.
Not fears, doubts, worries, nor burdens.
Inhale, accept.
Exhale, surrender.
May your dreams be of peace
And when the new day arises may it be
Filled with hope
And the promise of chances to take and change to embrace.
Sleep well.
Good night.

Evening 248.

Do not shun the night;
Its darkness and silence
Are not meant to stir loneliness
Or to weave wearied thoughts
Into doubt-ridden tangles.
The night is not a time to gather regrets about us as a cold
blanket
But a time to let them go;
Not a time to let unbidden sadness overwhelm us,
But a time to release sadness and open our hearts
In thankfulness for new moments, new chances,
New perceptions and understandings.
It is a time to be enfolded in the warm and gentle blanket of
Forgiveness,
Hope,
Healing,
And renewal.
Now, then, in the graceful arms of evening may you
Sleep well, friend.
Good night.

Evening 249.

Back porch, quiet breeze, flashing fireflies,
Scents of summer grass and warm ponds,
Fluttering birds in trees, unseen in the darkness.
The night calls the world to rest,
To put down the worries of the day and find
Comfort in darkness, in shadows, in silence.
Beneath the silver stars and the golden moon,
Find the peace you seek.
The peace you deserve.
And sleep well.

Evening 250.

Moments, as steady and certain as our heartbeats,
As our breaths,
Carry us forward, ever forward,
From day to twilight to evening;
Never backward, never into the past, but onward,
Onward.
Heartbeats,
Breaths,
What is becomes what was in the blink of an eye;
Memories to cherish or release into forgetfulness.
Be in the now, this dark, gentle, shadowed moment,
Feel it, savor it, and accept its gift of sleep;
Surrender.
From evening to midnight to pre-dawn;
Never backward, but onward,
Healed now, renewed,
Rise up into the morning and the
Next moment that awaits
For us to feel, to savor, to explore, to learn from,
To carry on.

Evening 251.

Bare feet, heavy lids,
We are the same when sleep comes
To humble and heal.

Evening 252.

Night's wind, a muted flute's song through the trees;
Chorus of rustling grasses,
Insects not yet gone to bed.
Shadows blend into one, a gentle cloak laid down upon the land
By evening's certain hand,
Stirring lanterns and stars to life.
Pulsing heartbeats of those who arise at the setting of the sun
And those who withdraw in the darkness to rest.
Sleep, then, friends, if sleep you desire.
May you find peace, healing,
Comfort, and renewal.
Good night.
Good night.

Evening 253.

Surrender to the softness of evening, to the deepness of sleep, and rise into healing as the sun rises on the wings of joy.

Evening 254.

Night is here, stepping in quietly, gently,
With a smile and a nod,
Urging us as we lie down to rest to recall
The kindness we offered another during the day,
Or the kindness offered to us from another.
Let us think on this, and hold it as a soft blanket against our
hearts;
Let us know the joy that compassion brings
To the mind and soul.
Yet if there was no kindness given nor received,
Let us think on this as well, and find contentment in knowing
That once the darkness has receded and the morning has
returned
There lies before us countless chances to reach out and
Be an active participant in the sharing of compassion and
understanding.
In that knowledge sleep deeply
And sleep well.
Good night, friend.
Good night.

Evening 255.

Kind-faced moon, smiling stars,
Watchful companions in the vast, satin sky.
Whispering softly,
Inviting you to join the dance of the night.
Shadows lift you and rock you gently.
Your heart beats in rhythm with the music of dreams,
You spirit sings you to sleep.

Evening 256.

Weary, needing rest,
Exhale the day, let it go,
Inhale the night. Sleep.

Evening 257.

Night's hand is not heavy, but insistent;
Day's journey is over,
Turn your burdens over to the darkness,
Release your doubts to the quiet.
What you need come morning will be in good keeping;
What you do not need will be gone,
Faded like mist in the warmth of the shimmering sun.
Therefore do not worry,
Do not fret.
Let the healing touch of the evening comfort you
And the certain, sacred reason for your being reassure you.
Good night, friend.
Good night.

Evening 258.

Evening star, irrepressible, confident,
Clouds pewter soft and drifting,
Benevolent moon peers down at the Earth
As darkness overcomes the land with a gentle power
That calls us to rest.
Give up the struggle,
Surrender to the peace that awaits you
In the mighty, merciful arms of the sacred night.
Sleep deeply.
Sleep well.
Be healed.

Evening 259.

Sometimes the night feels cold and hard. However is not the night that is callus, but our sadness or worries that cling to us in the darkness. Be in the moment, therefore, for the moment is soft and kind. It asks that we let go of grief or anxiety; it urges us to breathe, deeply, and slowly, acknowledging each breath as Divine CPR that will unburden our hearts and carry us forward into sleep. A gentle, healing sleep. Good night, friend.

Evening 260.

A rose is no less a rose in the shadows, a river no less a river in the darkness. What may be lost to sight at night is not reduced from what it was in the light of day. A smile, a nod of encouragement, a hand outstretched in friendship. Likewise, that which is within is unchanged even the sun fades and the moon rises, even as energy wanes and the need to rest draws you down into dreams. Hope remains hope, courage remains courage, accomplishments remain accomplishments. You remain you. Love remains love. Sleep now, and be renewed. Blessings to you.

Evening 261.

Evening whispers a bedtime story,
A never-ending, star-bright tale of time rolling into eternity,
A beautiful flowing
Of what was, what is,
And what will surely be;
Moving fearlessly, peacefully forward.
Be still, and listen.
Hear your name spoken in the story,
A hero of your life,
Where you should be in this very moment,
Moving forward with it all,
A player in the eternal
That Which Is.
A soul whose presence makes the world
All the more right for being here,
All the more wonderful for what you offer.
Sleep well, now, dear friend.
Be still,
And find the fearless peace that
Awaits you in the arms of the night.

Evening 262.

The day that is behind is behind,
Gone with the setting sun,
And the moment that is here is what is.
You cannot go back to change what has occurred
Nor wish into existence an alternative past.
Do not, then, burden yourself with sadness or regrets;
Take what has been learned,
But do not cling to what was.
Move into the night,
Grateful for the gentle darkness and for rest;
Grateful for new moments
That present themselves as certainly
As the ticking of the clock,
The glowing of the moon,
And the shining of the smiling stars.
Sleep, now,
And be renewed.
Good night.

Evening 263.

Good night, friend. May your mind quiet, and may the peaceful music of your soul sing you to sleep.

Evening 264.

Let the starlight find your heart,
And moonlight fill your spirit;
Let gentle sounds of the night lull you to sleep
With soft, orchestral voices
That have sung lullabies to the Earth
Since time began.
Now is your time,
Your place in history,
You are here,
Part of everything that is now
And rightly so.
Know this.
Let go of fear
And pride,
Arrogance
And doubt,
Anger
And regrets.
Release them to the past.
Find peace under the
Starlight,
The moonlight
And sleep well.

Evening 265.

How many turns of the Earth to live? How many risings of the pumpkin sun and comings of night-red clouds? How many dawns or twilights, noondays or midnights? Awakenings and sleepings? No one can know and no soul can tell. Life is as it is, precious and personal, unfolding, growing, grasping, touching, becoming. Perhaps it finds joy in that which is but a hair's breath away; perhaps it leaps with boundless determination for the stars. A day, then? A night? A year or one thousand? Time is not the final judge of value, but merely a ticking clock that amuses itself on the wall. Life is as it is. Precious. Personal. Embrace it, honor it. And with the certainty of your importance and that of the lives around you, take leave of this day and sleep. Sleep well. Good night, dear friend.

Evening 266.

Silver moonlight dances
Upon the waves of the lake;
Dance, too, in your dreams.

Evening 267.

Weight upon your shoulders,
Burdens on your mind,
Seek to overwhelm you,
Seek to make you blind
To all the peace around you
As certain at the moon,
As brilliant as the starlight,
As kind as dusk in June.
As strong as mountain forests,
As calm as shadows dark,
As real as winds of winter
And the singing of a lark.
Un-shoulder heavy weights, then,
And free your burdened mind,
Let your soul embrace
The peace you're meant to find.
Give up your regrets now,
And toss your doubts away,
Then sleep a blessed, healing sleep
Until the dawning day.

Evening 268.

Nocturnal creatures chirr in the trees. Night breezes stir the grass. A crescent moon glows softly in the blackness, silent and gentle. Sleep well, friend. And may your dreams be gentle and sweet.

Evening 269.

River of night,
Flowing steadily,
Surely through the darkness,
Keeping pace with the sparkling stars
And patient moon,
Will lift us,
Carry us effortlessly
From dusk
Through midnight
And into the mist of pre-dawn,
Washing away the grit of one day
That we might be strengthened and ready
To rise into the next.
Let go;
Drift with the river.
Sleep in peace and
Gratitude.
Good night.

Evening 270.

Quiet night,
Speak in whispers;
Gentle breeze,
Sing softest songs.
Shadows dark and still,
Bring gifts of peace,
That calm our hearts
Amid the storm.
We shall free our spirits
To fly beyond,
High into eternal realms,
Where gratitude
And joy are one,
And there we find
Healing, acceptance awaits.
Sleep then,
And sweet may your dreaming be,
Washing away
Despair and fear.
Cradled in
Arms of the Divine,
Safe, sure,
Tended perfectly through silent darkness
Into the rising sun.

Evening 271.

Heartbeats, steady, sure,
Awake through the swirling night
As you, in peace, sleep.

Evening 272.

Even when winds blows wild across the lake, the water beneath the surface remains still and calm. Even as clouds whirl and twist and cover the face of the moon, the moon is not changed. Even as darkness comes over the land and chases the sun's light away, that which is there upon the land is unmoved and untroubled. Even as restless night worries churn our thoughts, there is a stillness and clarity under it all, a soul in each of us that holds steady and sure. Breathe easily, then, and look inside to find the peace that is yours. Release the doubts and regrets. Remember the good that is you, and rest well in that certainty. Good night, friend. Sleep well.

Evening 273.

Day reveals the things of sight; night reveals things of the heart, things of the deepest purpose, things unbound, free, and loving.

Evening 274.

Listen to the silence of the night
And feel the silence within.
For it is there, in the quiet darkness,
That hope and contentment will grow
And the beautiful wonder of life will return.

Evening 275.

Lightning,
Brilliant rage,
Flashing across
A blackened sky;
Ragged, furious energy slashing the fabric
Of the night
Over and
Over again.
Look! See! Feel!
Its power demands,
Awes, humbles,
Draws us up within ourselves,
Knotted, anxious.
Yet wait;
In patience let it be,
Let it happen,
For its energy will soon be spent;
The darkness will enfold and calm the fury.
Those things that are angry and temporary will be done,
Blown away on an evening's gentle breath.
That which is peaceful and eternal will remain.
And so it is for us,
Caught up in ragged wrath,
That slashes the fabric of our souls,
Over and
Over again.
Its power demands,
Awes, humbles,
Drawing us up within ourselves,
Knotted, anxious.
Yet wait;
In patience let it be,
For the rage will soon be spent;
That which is true and eternal

Will rise up, enfold, and calm the storm.
That which is angry and temporary will be done;
The breath of stillness will blow the angst away
And bless our spirits with peace.
Sleep well, then, friend.
Sleep deeply.
And heal.
Good night.

Evening 276.

Silvery stars sweep the skies,
Scattered across the Universe in their perfect places,
Sparkling notes of the vast and awesome score,
The symphony of the Universe.
And all of us, intricate parts,
All of us with our unique verses
To sing, to offer, to breathe, to live.
Each heartbeat the rhythm,
Each utterance, a lyric.
Each day a chorus,
Each night, a bridge.
Rest now within music of eternity,
Sleep well to the lullaby of the Divine.
Silvery stars sweep the skies,
Scattered across the Universe in their perfect places,
Sparkling notes of the vast and awesome score,
The symphony of the Universe.
And all of us, intricate parts,
All of us with our unique verses
To sing, to offer, to breathe, to live.
Each heartbeat the rhythm,
Each utterance, a lyric.
Each day a chorus,
Each night, a bridge.
Rest now within music of eternity,
Sleep well to the lullaby of the Divine.

Evening 277.

Exhausted, defeated, depleted
From the frets and doubts of the day.
Sensing an aloneness,
That clings to the spirit;
A vague sadness that will not fade.
Here is the night once more,
Offering silence and stillness,
A time to release your fears.
To open to
The gentle arms of darkness,
The compassionate gaze of the stars,
The understanding smile of the moon.
Let it go.
Let it be.
Surrender.
Rest.
Sleep well, friend.
Good night.

Evening 278.

Life is embroidered
One day into another into another,
A strong, delicate thread of time into a
Tapestry of memory and experience.
Stitches of gold and gray,
Emerald and pewter,
Sage and scarlet and ebony,
Fog and snow,
Sun and rain.
Patterns of growth and resistance,
Joy and regrets,
Swirling designs exuberant with energy;
Static lines that fold into themselves,
Hesitant, afraid.
As night arrives, and the time has come to rest,
Put down your handiwork;
Let the peaceful darkness pull free the tangled stitches
That disrupt the pattern you created today.
Let the gentle shadows unravel that
Which you did not mean to add,
Giving your heart a clearer focus,
Your tapestry fresh space on which, tomorrow,
You shall create something beautiful.
Tomorrow,
A new day to think more clearly,
Act more kindly,
Feel more deeply,
Love more completely,
Forgive more freely both yourself and those around you.
And now sleep
A deep and healing sleep.
Good night.

Evening 279.

Desiderata says, "You are a child of the Universe, no less than the trees or stars; you have a right to be here." Do not doubt it. As day gives way to night, as sunlight graciously steps back for evening to take its place, rest assured that nothing exists that is not meant to exist. There is a purpose for everything, for everyone. Take heart, also, that each new moment offers a newness of life, offers chances never seen before, offers hope both true and bright. Sleep then, and sleep well into the morning, dear soul.

Evening 280.

Be patient with the night,
Its silence and stillness,
Its distant stars and misty moon.
Let the time roll as it will,
Slowly along the ticking clock;
Do not long for it to rush past,
To be gone and done.
Open to the silence,
Breathe in the calm,
Accept the peace offered by the gentle darkness,
And the gift of healing that awaits.
Be patient, also, with yourself,
Let go of expectations and disappointments;
Breathe out the anxiety of the day past,
Accept the peace that resides in your soul
And sleep deeply within the arms of the gentle darkness.
Good night.

Evening 281.

Night is the friend of day,
A partner in the flow of time,
Holding hands to create the
Eternal link,
The never-ending reality
Of which you are part,
A beautiful earth-bound star.
Lift your face and look up!
Welcome the peace that nighttime brings;
Breathe in the quiet.
Feel the gentle embrace.
Accept that you are right and good,
Tasked with a purpose as unique and lovely
As the misted diamonds of the Milky Way
And the drifting reflection of a smiling moon
Upon a steel-dark lake.

Evening 282.

The same vast, dark sky overhead,
The same firefly stars winking happily;
The same chalk moon stamped upon the fabric of the night,
And the same strong winds falling, rising, encircling.
The same grand Earth beneath our feet,
The same seas rushing against our shores,
The same mountains holding clouds aloft,
And the same chirring of life,
Insistent, invasive,
Beautiful.
Here we are, then,
Each and every one of us,
Beneath the vast, dark sky,
The firefly stars and chalk moon;
Here we are, the same in need,
In hopes and fears,
Doubts and joys,
Struggles and failures.
The same in grief and longing,
Hopelessness and glorious power.
None less than another but all wonderfully human
And wonderfully right;
United in our commonalities,
Comforted in the certainty that
In the Eye of that Which Is,
We are intended,
We are full of promise,
We are worthy.
And now, as the stars shift and the moon yawns,
We are called to rest, to sleep,
To regain strength and peace of mind.
So that when the sun rises,
We will step into the dawning day,
Ready for what comes next.

Evening 283.

Hear the gentle voice,
Deep in your soul, whispering,
Sleep, precious one. Sleep.

Evening 284.

These are the voices of the evening – rumbles of a distant train, faint harmonies of birds as they wrangle then settle amid the shadowed trees, slippers scuffing across a floor, a television talking to itself, a clock humming on a wall, a cat's purr, a dishwasher gurgling, deep sighs, rustling blankets, creaking bed. Now, as you let go of the day and surrender to the night, let its voices ease your mind, calm your worries, and whisper you to a peaceful sleep. Good night, friend. Good night.

Evening 285.

Follow your dreams into the night,
Through the shadows, freely,
Dancing from moon to star
To touch eternity,
And laugh in harmony with all that was,
Is, and will be,
Freed from troubles,
Released from worries
Part of it all,
And joyous in the being.

Evening 286.

Day bushes her fingertips along the grasses,
Washes of gold across a field of jade,
Retreating so that night may step in
And gather the land and all its creatures
Within its gentle embrace.
And now, amid the deepening shadows,
Release the troubles of your heart;
Surrender to the soft song of darkness.
Feel its peace surround you,
Comfort and calm you.
You are safe.
You are blessed.
Rest well, friend.
Rest well.

Evening 287.

A half-read book upon a shelf,
A crumb upon a plate,
A shoe upended on the floor,
A houseplant left to fate.
A towel hung on the shower door,
A sock curled like a slug,
A pillow in a light blue case,
A hole the puppy dug.
A door that squeals when it is shut,
A teacup in the sink,
A fridge in need of cleaning out,
A clock long out of sync.
A cricket chirping on the porch,
A toothbrush in a cup,
A rug with stains that won't come out,
A blind that won't stay up.
Simple things around, about,
Things we overlook,
Tidbits that make up a life,
That crumb, that towel, that book.
So, as the sun gives up her hold
And disappears from view,
As darkness takes his rightful place,
And night has come, anew,
Let's be thankful, grateful for
The details, large and small,
Things that when our lives are done,
We'll wistfully recall.
As we close our eyes tonight
And shadows gather, deep,
Let gratitude for all there is
Sing our souls to sleep.

Evening 288.

Gentle, ageless moon,
Certain, vigilant, steady;
My soul, be at peace.

Evening 289.

Night is here,
Spread out before us,
A soft bed fashioned of
Darkness, gentleness, and the
Soothing sounds of the Earth.
Hear the breath of the breeze,
The heartbeat of the sea,
The murmurings of life as it calms
And quiets to rest.
Lie down, now, in the place that awaits you,
The place where no words are needed,
Where regrets drift away on the evening air
And the blanket of reassurance enfolds you,
Holds you.
Be at peace.
Sleep well.
Good night.

Evening 290.

The moon does not fret over his reflective role,
And the stars do not argue over their placements in the
Universe.
Evening's shadows do not hesitate to spread across the land,
Nor question their purpose in the rhythm of time.
Likewise the sun does not question the Earth as she turns her
face away
Yet again to rest peacefully in the darkness.
And you, child of the Earth, do not doubt your role,
Your placement, your purpose in this, your time.
It is as certain as daybreak, as lovely as dusk,
As noble as the steadfast moon in a midnight sky.
In this be assured, be comforted;
In this, release your cares and doubts to the past
And welcome the healing that awaits you in sleep.

Evening 291.

Breath of the night,
Deep, cleansing,
Softly, gently given and accepted
From the Earth to us
Then given back again;
As rhythmic as heartbeats,
As silent as shooting stars,
As powerful as the life it nurtures.
Count your breaths as you wait to sleep,
Slowly, gratefully, respectfully;
They will keep and sustain you
As you surrender to the darkness,
To the quiet,
To the peace.

Evening 292.

As evening's shadows gather
And the world has gone to bed,
As you hold your child or kitten,
Your pillow or your wife,
As you hold your husband, your lover,
Your blanket, or your memories,
The gentle night is holding you.
It encompasses you,
Surrounds you.
Feel its stillness,
Accept its comfort,
Surrender to its strength;
Let all worries fly away as sparks
From a dying ember,
And be at peace.

Evening 293.

Even if the night feels angry, it is not. Even when you feel weak, you are not. Even if you sense there is no light within you, know that there are those around you who see your light, who look to it, and who are relieved to see it shining in the darkness.

Evening 294.

Is there anything happier than a flowing stream
Or more content than a glowing star?
More at home than a nesting bird
Or more at peace than a resting child?
Dear one, seek your own happiness;
Claim contentment,
Find your home in the peace of evening.
Turn thoughts of sorrow and regret from your heart's door
And drift joyfully on dreams from nighttime's shore.

Evening 295.

When the lights go down on the world, when we can't see what lies ahead and life feels hard and strange and sad, know that there is Hope. Every new moment offers the possibility of change, every new second the gift of transformation. Each star attests to this. Each dancing firefly. Each rustle of an evening breeze through a field. Each ripple of moonlight on a pond. And so as you release the day and surrender to the night, feel the Hope. Breathe the Hope. Pray the Hope. Imagine the Hope. Know the Hope. For you are the Hope. Rest well, now, in the peaceful darkness. Sleep deeply and surely in the arms of evening. And come the rising sun, rise also, and share the Hope. Good night, friend. Good night.

Evening 296.

Day withdraws, rolling up the carpet of light
And taking it with her until tomorrow,
Leaving the softness of evening in its place.
Colors fade, shadows grow;
Stillness parts the curtain of the sky to
Reveal the great, unimaginable wonders beyond.
What a beautiful time this is,
What a gift of relief and peace;
A divine embrace of the soul,
A glorious benediction for the spirit.
Lie down now, we of tired shoulders,
Wearied minds, and tasks undone.
Breathe deeply of the night.
Rejoice in the reality of the moment,
The vastness of creation,
And the certainty that we are here
Because we are supposed to be here.
Then let go,
Surrender,
Drift away into healing.
Sleep well, friend.
Sleep well.

Evening 297.

Gather together
Thoughts of forgiveness, kindness;
Hold them close, and sleep.

Evening 298.

Moth on a window screen,
Lace-winged and whisper soft.
Porch light lifts its timid voice to
Sing with the noble stars
In silent harmony.
A breeze, cooled by darkness,
Passes gently through grasses,
Affectionately caressing,
Moving on.
Bare feet on carpet,
Beneath cool sheets;
Pillow welcomes,
The night embraces.
Breath of troubles exhaled,
Breath of calm inhaled.
Gentle dreams to you.
Sleep well.
Good night.

Evening 299.

For the heart that keens in darkness,
The spirit that mourns at night,
The soul beat down and weary,
And the one who hides from sight;
Know you're not forgotten,
That hope will breathe once more,
As certain as the moon above
Rains moonlight on the floor,
As sure as trees stand tall and true
And rivers seek the sea,
Your trembling soul and saddened heart
Will rise up, strong and free.
So give yourself to sleeping,
And the healing it will bring,
When comes the shining morning,
Arise once more, and sing.

Evening 300.

Follow the growing darkness,
The shadowed trail lined with diamond-stars and fireflies,
Beneath benedictive arms of gentle trees,
Along evening's ebony brook to the sea
Where your dreams wait to carry you into sleep.
Let go, surrender, step out.
Drift on, then,
Beyond the shore of worry and regret,
Far from despair and fear
And into the calm, benevolent peace of night.
Rest well, friend.
Rest well.

Evening 301.

Intricate etchings, black and deep
Against a charcoal sky;
Layered branches hold aloft the Universe
And the silver-dust of countless scattered stars.
Look up, look long,
For you belong to this.

Evening 302.

In the still of the evening,
All seek their places of rest;
Birds, the deep, sheltering arms of trees;
Rabbits, their dark, cool burrows;
Deer, the dense and leafy brush;
Dogs, a mat by a crackling fire;
Cats, the well-warmed spot beside their masters.
Seek, now, your own place of rest,
A soft bed and pillow for the body,
A sweet dream for the spirit,
And the renewal of joy and peace for the soul.
Good night, friend.
Good night.

Evening 303.

Close the curtain, still the light,
Gone the daytime, here the night,
Evening breezes gentle, calm,
Darkness gifts its soothing balm.
Those who grieve and those who weep
Surrender to a healing sleep;
Though your heart be crossed with pain
And all the Earth seems drenched in rain,
As your sadness, heavy, lies,
Upon your spirit, 'neath the skies,
Know that all around you, still,
Though deep the river, high the hill,
Kindness and compassion flow,
As surely as the grasses grow.
As certain as the moon on high,
As true as evening birds that fly,
Tender mercies from above
Reach out to hold you with their love.
Tears will come but peace shall, too,
As turns the world into the new.

Evening 304.

A star in the vast, dark Universe is set in its rightful place in its rightful time; it shines brilliantly, beautifully with a power from within. It does not will itself to shine nor force itself to shine, for its glow is intrinsic; it is what makes it a star. So are you set in your rightful place in this time, this life, shining brilliantly with a power from within. Even when you do not sense it, it shines; even when you doubt it, it shines; even at your weakest, it shines. It is intrinsic; you do not need to will it nor force it into being. It is what makes you. It is the greatest part of you. Knowing this, let go of regrets to which you cling. Release the fear of what might be. Look inward and see the glow that the world sees. Know the innate rightness that is you. Then, comforted, surrender to the evening, to the vast, dark Universe, and find peace in sleep. Good night, friend. Good night.

Evening 305.

May peace descend upon you like the gentle light of the moon, and may sleep enfold you like the sweet shadows of evening.

Evening 306.

Heavenly canvas awash with the stuff of eternity,
A glorious artwork created
Of stars and moonlight, hopes and prayers.
Wise and silent, vigilant and patient,
We are watched from above even as we watch from below,
The Divine gazing upon the Earthly,
And the Earthly, while looking up,
Discover with awe and a rush of wonder
That we, too, come from the Divine,
And that the heavenly canvas and glorious eternal scene
Shall be our inheritance.

Evening 307.

As gentle as moon-glow
And dear as starlight,
May evening shadows surround you,
Hold you,
And remind you that
All is well.
With each new moment and
Each new breath,
Life is renewed,
Hope is rekindled,
Strength is restored.
Sleep well, then, friend.
Sleep well.

Evening 308.

Soft pillow, cool sheets,
Favorite pj's, heartbeats,
Clock's tick, moon's glow,
Stars arise for evening's show.
Weary mind, velvet sky,
Heavy eyelids, peaceful sigh.
Purring cat, shadows deep,
Curl up now, it's time to sleep.

Evening 309.

Night is here and our work is done, yet something within us wants to rush forward into tomorrow, to see what it holds, to try it out, to brace ourselves, to prepare the defenses we fear we might need to take on and conquer the day. Give it thought, yes, and make the plan. But then step back. Let go. Let us free ourselves from the specters of what might be and find the tranquility in what is. In the quiet shadows of this moment, in the blessed stillness. In the steadfast stars that hold place above us and the precious world that holds place beneath us. Breathe in the peace that is offered and breathe out uncertainty and doubt. And then sleep well, my friend.

Evening 310.

Gentle, steady River of Time,
Bearing away that which was,
Our doubts and pains,
Our fumblings and fears;
Washing the grit of regret
From this moment
That we may see clearly
To find joy, hope, and peace.
Sleep now, dear friend,
Calm and comforted.
Be renewed in rest;
Drift along the certain and gentle River of Time
Into a new morning,
A new day,
A new chance to begin again.

Evening 311.

Soft the carpet,
Soft the sigh,
The moonlight pale on the yard
And the vague wash of the Milky Way across the sky.
Soft the whisper,
Soft the blanket,
The chirring of katydids upon the shadowed hill
And the breeze against the night-dark grasses.
Soft the smile,
Soft the grateful heart,
The gentle, comforting arms of evening
And the blessed sleep that awaits.

Evening 312.

Here we are in evening's hour,
When sunlight fades and shadows flower,
Colors quiet, tired eyes close,
Voices soften, darkness grows;
Hold at heart, now, our dear ones,
Fathers, mothers, daughters, sons,
Friends and lovers, husbands, wives,
Whom, throughout our busy lives
Bless us with their steadfast love
As sure as silvered stars above;
As strong as waves upon a shore,
As grand as brilliant birds that soar,
Gentle, patient, caring, true,
So familiar, ever new.
Now that night has come once more,
And sleep awaits to heal, restore,
Make thankfulness our quiet sigh
And gratitude our lullaby.

Evening 313.

The world will take care of its business as you sleep;
Breezes will blow,
Owls will soar amid the midnight trees of the forests,
Cattle will wander and graze even in the darkness;
Crickets will chirr, moths will dance,
Waves will splash against the shore,
Rivers will flow and
Porch lights and campfires will blaze.
Even the Earth beneath you will continue to turn,
Joyously,
A carousel of life.
So let go and find rest,
For what needs doing is being done,
And that which requires your touch
Can wait.
Good night.
Pleasant dreams, friend.

Evening 314.

Worries, be gone now,
My friends are tired and need sleep;
Nighttime, comfort them.

Evening 315.

May the peace of darkness,
The silence of the lake,
The certainty of stars,
The steadfastness of the river,
The serenity of the moon,
The kindness of trees,
The forgiveness of the moment,
And the compassion of God, however you may conceive Him
to be,
Surround you, comfort you, hold you,
And ease your sorrows so that you will sleep,
Sleep well,
And when morning comes you will rise up healed,
Renewed,
And opened to the gift of joy.
Good night, friend.
Good night.

Evening 316.

The day ends with evening's onset
And the night concludes as day arises.
Day into night into day,
Sunlight into moonlight,
Star-glow into day-glow,
Time flowing, a river that carries us all
Forward, onward.
How impossible to go backward,
How sad to stand in place.
What relief to move into new moments,
New possibilities,
New insights,
New chances.
Do not cling to the river's edge nor
Hold with anxious fingers to the now.
Release,
Welcome the journey,
For ahead lie dreams and goals and unknown wonders.
And so now,
With time having directed us into
Another beautiful night,
Let us welcome it
And be grateful for it;
For the sleep that awaits,
For the rest and healing it offers,
And for the wakefulness that will follow
With new possibilities,
New insights,
New chances.

Evening 317.

Rise up into the night,
Upon the breath of the wind,
High into the jubilant darkness
To dance among the stars and the mists of eternity,
And into dreams that await;
Dreams of wonder and freedom,
Of possibilities and imagination,
Of wisdom and healing,
Of all that can be and should be.
Rise up within the arms of sleep
And into the wonder of what you need,
What you hope for, what you pray for.
Rise up.
Rise up into Peace.
Rise up into Joy.

Evening 318.

One breath into the next,
One note into another,
Onward into dusk, nightfall,
Evening, midnight;
One heartbeat into the next.
One sigh into another,
The moon crests the darkness and moves on
As the Earth turns beneath the brilliantly-black sky.
One tick of the clock into the next,
One moment into another,
Never ceasing,
Ever glorious, birthed anew,
Onward, leaving the past behind.
Find peace, then,
And hope and joy.
Let go of what was and surrender to the night,
To the quiet gentleness of now,
Sleep well, and ride into morning
On the restful whisper of peace.

Evening 319.

Bare feet, soft rug,
Tired smile, night's hug,
Darkness falls,
Sleep calls,
Blankets, sheets,
Pillow greets;
Drifting dreams,
Moonbeam streams,
Stars' light,
Good night.

Evening 320.

Feel the smiling night,
Joyous to know and hold you;
Feel its peace. Sleep well.

Evening 321.

Tremulous spirit, do not fear,
Wearied soul, you are safe;
You have climbed the mountain of day,
And have reached the summit of evening.
It is time to rest.
Shed your worries now;
Surrender that which has broken your heart,
Caused you concern,
Or weighed you down.
Let out the breath of doubt and draw in the breath of peace.
There is goodness around you,
And the shadows of night offer their silent benediction.

Evening 322.

Night is here. It is time to release the burdens of the day. Let sleep rise up, enfold us, and carry us gently forward. May we remember, as we drift into our slumber, that regardless of past stumblings and struggles, we are the heroes of our lives, of our time and place. We are important to this world. Therefore, as we awaken in the morning, refreshed, stronger, let us open more than our eyes to the light of the sun. Let's open our hearts to each other. Good night, friend. Good night.

Evening 323.

Even if the night feels heavy,
A weight upon your shoulders,
Even when the darkness seems lonely
And the moon appears to turn its face away,
All is not lost.
Nothing good has gone.
Look inward, then, for the light that burns,
A light of soul and spirit and possibilities and hope.
You are no less than you ever were,
But only weary and doubtful.
In the silence seek the light within,
Search for it with a whisper of gratitude
And an attitude of reverence
And you will find it,
Burning steadily and as brightly as it ever was.
Then, wearied and comforted
Sleep,
Sleep well, friend.
Good night.

Evening 324.

The night in its silence is beautiful, a canvas on which you might paint a lovely dream, or a gentle artist who might paint your heart with hope and peace.

Evening 325.

Happy the topaz moon
To be created a moon,
And the opal stars
To shine as they are meant to shine.
Happy the tall and silent trees
To stand where they stand,
And happy the cold river to flow,
The mountains to hold white clouds aloft,
And the owl to grace the winds of night.
As day retreats into the shadows and evening enfolds you,
As stillness takes its place within the darkness,
May you find contentment in being
Who you are;
For no other reason were you made,
For no other reason are you here.
In being, then, may you find purpose;
In purpose may you find courage,
Strength,
Contentment,
Compassion,
Happiness, and
Peace.
May all this be yours as you gaze up at
The silver moon
And as the opal
Stars smile down upon you.

Evening 326.

May nothing disturb you this gentle night;
May no fears or troubles stand between you and
The sweet sleep that awaits.
Hold to the knowledge that fears withdraw before love,
And troubles shrink before goodness.
Then may your sleep be
Peaceful,
Unhindered,
And blessed.

Evening 327.

The circle has turned again. Light has given way to darkness, day has surrendered to night. Accept the peace the evening offers. Sleep well. Heal. Renew. And know that tomorrow waits with arms full of opportunities both large and small, all for you.

Evening 328.

Quiet, gentle breeze,
Breath of the Earth,
Sigh of the night,
Carry away the turmoil and frets of the day
That this, my friend, might rest well,
Might find the peace of being,
Might sleep a blessed and safe sleep
In the Arms of the Loving Divine.

Evening 329.

White flowers of night
Dotting the sky overhead,
Count them now, and sleep.

Evening 330.

Things you possess are no more you
Than a bird is its nest.
Things you do not possess are no more you
Than the space between stars are the stars, themselves.
Do not let impermanent trappings define you
Nor let petty expectations oppress you.
Your value lies exactly as it should be,
Equal among all,
Known by Eternity,
Loved by That Which Is.
In this knowledge, find peace.
In this certainty, know comfort.
Rest well, now, beneath the dark, velvet sky.
Good night, friend.
Good night.

Evening 331.

Eternal music,
Melody of day to night;
Song of life, play on.

Evening 332.

Shadows grow long in the city,
Blanketing building and street,
Swirling amid cabs and buses,
Pooling 'round city folks' feet.

Growing with each passing moment,
Claiming what's rightfully theirs,
Painting the alleys and doorways,
Climbing the porches and stairs.

Streetlights join the celebration,
Bright headlights pattern the roads,
People go home from their labors,
Soon to un-shoulder their loads.

Welcome the new coming night hours,
Be glad as the darkness moves in,
Let's capture the joy of the star-rise
And delight in the moon's charming grin.

Then as the full evening surrounds us,
As all that is near bids us sleep,
May we surrender our worries,
And claim rest that's tranquil and deep.

In the soft shadows of evening,
'Neath the sentinel stars and the moon,
May we find rest and find healing,
As night hums a sweet, peaceful tune.

Evening 333.

Shining stars,
Points of light in the eternity of the heavens,
Steady, certain, distant
Yet nestled deep within the human soul.
We touch them in our dreams and
Are touched by them in our imaginings.

Evening 334.

Sad heart, stung with life,
Cowed by circumstance and doubt,
Surrender to the night and its healing balm
Of quiet and stillness,
Of tranquility, and transition.
Let the calm of the moment surround and soothe you;
Know the peace that comes with the
Certainty of change,
And accept the steadfast love that lies above,
Below, beside, before, and within you.
Sleep now in the gentle, patient darkness;
Rest well into tomorrow,
When things begin new again
And strength will fill your heart.

Evening 335.

Great sea of Night,
Gentle waves of shadow and wonderment,
Rushing silently, steadily upon the shores of our hearts,
Bringing dreams and hopes
And washing away residues of fear and regret,
Touching spirits with star-lit fingers
And bidding us a soothing, peaceful sleep.

Evening 336.

Night follows day, and winter comes after fall. Streams flow into rivers, and oceans give up themselves to the clouds. Change is certain, a blessing from nature. Rest well, then, knowing that peace follows uncertainty and strength will, indeed, rise up out of weariness.

Evening 337.

Fading daylight,
Soft breaths slowing,
Rising shadows,
Cool streams flowing.
Bird wings, feathered,
Whispered, beating,
Flecks of moonlight
On lakes, fleeting.
Tender lovers
Gently holding,
Prayerful fingers,
Hopeful, folding.
Wistful memories
Blessed in keeping;
Precious souls now
Peaceful, sleeping.

Evening 338.

The road does not turn back upon itself, and rightly so. Therefore, as you lay your head upon your night-soft pillow and turn out the light, do not let your worries pull you into the past. Rather consider this very moment, this time and place in which you lie. Sense the bed beneath you. Feel the sheets, the blanket, the air that surrounds and sustains you, the soft sounds of the night. Release what came before. And know that in the morning, you shall set off on a new road filled with new hopes, new choices, and new chances. And so rest. Rest well, friend.

Evening 339.

Sweet bells of the night,
Ringing in the human heart,
Calling us to rest.

Evening 340.

As you lie down at the end of the day
And thoughts whirl and collide with each other
Like so many pale, anxious moths
Against the brilliance of a porch light,
Remember this.
You do not have to do it all.
You do not have to have it all.
You do not have to be it all.
Let go. Surrender.
Free your heart to tranquility and contentment.
For you are not meant to bear it all,
To have it all,
To be it all.
Rather you are meant to grow, to learn,
To experience, to share, and to love.
That is enough of a task for any of us.
Your shoulders are not wide enough for the world,
But are big enough for many of the tasks you face.
And when you find they are not
Reach out to others who, like you,
Are here to grow, to learn,
To experience, and to love.
Knowing this, be at peace.
Knowing this, sleep well,
Dear friend.
Sleep well.

Evening 341.

Drifting clouds at dusk,
Blushing, fragile gardens, reflecting the glory of
The setting sun;
Scarlet, umber,
Rose and coral.
Peaceful, unhurried,
Misted veils across a rising chalk-white moon.
Drifting, peaceful, unhurried,
Relinquishing the day and
Settling into sleep.
My day-weary friend, you are as dear as the clouds,
And as precious as the eternal, darkening sky.
And now, as dusk gives way to night,
Relinquish the day and
Find your well-deserved, peaceful rest
Beneath the silvery sand-spot moon and the
Fading gardens of evening's clouds.

Evening 342.

I am the darkness that has gathered
To surround you
With the coming of night;
Here to gently hold you, to comfort you;
Bid by my Creator to this purpose.
Kind, without judgment or scorn,
Strong and sure.
Sleep now, dear one.
Sleep deeply and well
While I keep watch.

Evening 343.

Evening is a gentle hand upon the heart, a gentle kiss upon the cheek, bidding us rest, calling us to close our eyes. Let go, and feel the sweet surrender that carries us into the healing peace of sleep.

Evening 344.

Midnight stands, proud and silent,
Between one day and the next.
Not a witching hour nor a time of fear,
But rather a moment that asks us
To shake the dust of the past from our feet
And move on, to step over
Into peace,
Into sleep, and
Into the newness that awaits upon rising.
Good night, friend.
Good night.

Evening 345.

The day is busy, bold, and bright,
Then comes the quiet, kindly night;
It whispers, "Time, dear one, to rest;
Let peace dwell deep within the breast.
Time to feel what is to feel,
To sort illusion from what's real.
To know the past is in the past
And what is based in love will last.
Time to let your worries fly
To vanish far beyond the sky.
To find, once more, the gentleness
That comes with evening's soft caress.
Put aside your woes and fears
And wipe away your anxious tears.
Sleep is here, now close your eyes;
Rest, friend, 'til it's time to rise."

Evening 346.

Open your hands.
Open your heart.
Open your spirit.
Close your eyes.
Good night, dear friend.
Sleep well.

Evening 347.

Into the forest, across the field,
Along the river, past the lake,
On the hillside, up the mountain,
Through the mist that shrouds the night.
In our dreaming, gently lifting,
Drifting high within the darkness,
Past the moon, around the stars,
Rise with joyous evening's light.
And now my friend
I bid you sleep,
And may your sleep
Be sweet and deep.

Evening 348.

Good night, friend. Sleep well, and know that tomorrow is a new day, a new beginning, and it is filled with more opportunities than we can imagine, if we just take the time to open our eyes and hearts.

Evening 349.

Onward we journey together, traveling as the world revolves night into day into night. Carried along by time; partnered with it to accomplish our goals and rise to our potentials. Let us not be anxious in our travels, grasping frantically for a fictional brass ring that, in the grasping, leaves us defeated and overwhelmed. Rather, we should seek the many golden chances to love, to share, and to be. Let us keep our hands and hearts open as we move from day to night into day, breathing in that which brings peace, breathing out that which causes fear. And, on the turn into evening, let us close our eyes and rest well. Let us sleep deeply. Let us dream dreams of kindness, courage, forgiveness, and hope.

Evening 350.

Tumbling leaves,
Waving grasses,
Darkening hillside,
Cooling breezes.
Growing shadows,
Melting sunlight,
Dimming rivers,
Scattering night birds.
Stretching kittens,
Yawning children,
Singing mothers,
Smiling fathers.
Covers rustling,
Eyelids closing,
Worries easing,
Troubles fading,
Night embracing,
Gently blessing,
Spirits rising
Set to dreaming.

Evening 351.

The night sky awakens,
Opening to reveal a gentle-faced moon,
The mists of eternity,
And a murmuration of stars
Swirling in unison;
Jubilant spirits
Celebrating their existence
And their purpose.
Lie down, now,
Beneath the sky
And the gentle, smiling moon.
Drift into sleep, rejoicing in your existence
And your certain place within the Universe
And the beautiful, swirling
Mists of eternity.

Evening 352.

We don't need to see
The moon to know it is there;
Know, too, love abides.

Evening 353.

The peace of the evening is here for the knowing,
Its calm for the taking,
And its healing for the accepting.
It is meant for you as much as
The pink-blue dawning, the mid-morn,
The noon-time and sun-bright afternoon.
The kindly night offers its cloak of stillness,
Its arms of darkness,
And its bed of gentleness
That you might sleep well
And sleep deeply.
Good night, friend.
Good night.

Evening 354.

Welcome the vulnerability that
Comes with evening's darkness;
Doors that open to our hidden fears,
Our dearest desires,
Our deepest doubts and fragile faiths,
Prayers offered, both answered and unanswered.
For with vulnerability comes relinquishing,
With relinquishing, newness;
With newness, healing,
With healing, hope,
With hope, comfort.
And now, my friend, may comfort surround you
And enfold you;
May hope rise up and shine from you as stars
Shine out from the depths of the
Glorious night.
Sleep well.
Sleep well.

Evening 355.

There are moments when words cannot suffice;
And so, in silence, look up at the vast, sea-black sky
With its joyful spatterings of crystal-stars,
And be filled the peace that exists beyond what can
Be spoken, thought,
Or expressed.

Evening 356.

Sing, silver-silent stars,
Sing this dear one to sleep;
For the day has been long and trying,
The tasks heavy and difficult.
Whisper, chalk-dust moon,
Whisper this precious spirit to rest.
For night is here, with offerings of
Stillness, patience, and recovery.
Surrender, sweet friend,
Surrender to the arms of gentle darkness
And drift into peaceful dreams,
Knowing that you are loved.

Evening 357.

Look upon yourself with the same compassion
That you offer the lost child,
The ailing old man,
The bullied teen,
The wounded fledgling,
The abandoned puppy.
Hold thoughts of yourself as tenderly and mercifully as this;
And then, beneath the grand, silent eternity of night's sky
Find peace,
Find healing,
And sleep.

Evening 358.

As day withdraws and darkness drifts across
Forest and field,
City and farm,
Town and hill,
Bringing shadows, stillness, and silence,
May those of us who live upon this dear Earth
Turn our thoughts from cares and doubts
To gratitude, forgiveness, and sweet thoughts
Of those we love.
Then may we sleep deeply
And sleep well
Within Divine Arms of Peace.

Evening 359.

Close your eyes and feel the night,
The calm, the still,
The gentle arms of darkness
Encircling you,
The quiet voice of shadows
Whispering,
"Let go. Surrender.
Sleep, and find healing."

Evening 360.

Rock gently
In a moon-soft breeze;
Drift through shadows,
Float on mists,
As sugar-bright stars sing you to sleep
And the cooling Earth
Opens her arms in a knowing
And gentle embrace.
Breathe out worries,
Breathe in peace, and
Rest my, friend.
Good night.

Evening 361.

Take each breath slowly;
Feel the heartbeats within you,
And welcome sleep.

Evening 362.

Come gentle evening
What should we keep
As shadows move in,
Silent and deep?
As soft eventide
Enfolds the land,
What should we draw close
To heart and hand?
Memories of sunshine,
Songs of the rain,
Leaves flying free,
Snow on the lane.
Stones in a river,
Friends on the phone,
Warm chocolate cookies,
Time spent alone.
Love and forgiveness,
Mercies received,
Kindness we've given,
A promise believed.
Rising of twilight,
Fireflies alight,
Thoughts of dear loved ones
In the dark, velvet night.
All of these, now,
Let us treasure and hold,
As eyes slowly close
And peaceful hands fold.

Evening 363.

Come tender night
What should we free
As stars light up
The dark sky's sea?
Beneath the kind moon's
Golden glow
What should we
Turn from and let go?
Fears that linger
In the heart
And doubts that
Tear our faith apart.
Thoughts that tell
Us not to try
And harsh regrets
That make us cry.
Angry words
That cut us deep
And burdens
That deny us sleep.
Do not keep them,
For their weight
Will only wound
And agitate.
The evening is for
Knowing peace
And finding
Joy in sweet release.
Let us claim
Our right to rest
And may our souls
Be gently blessed.
When comes the dawn

And we awake,
May we, healed,
Stand up, partake,
And then, renewed
By evening's balm,
Walk on, stand tall,
Strong, sure, and calm.

Evening 364.

Out among stars on the wings of night,
Finding solace and unity,
Knowing joy and freedom,
Soaring effortlessly through the darkness;
Surrendered to the moment
And needing nothing more.
With heart and hands open
To draw in the bliss, wisdom, and brilliant wonder
Of existence.
'Round and above,
Through and beneath,
Fearless,
Enraptured by the simplicity
And complexity of that which is.
Settling, quieting, waking,
Arising to carry the wisdom, freedom, and joy
Into the day.
May this be your dream in sleeping.
May this be your wonder in waking.
May this be your bliss in being.

Evening 365.

Life is as it will be,
Wondrous and uncertain,
Mysterious, familiar,
Beautiful, frightening,
Heartbreaking, enlightening, joyous.
Upon the ship of time we sail together,
Along smooth and storm-tossed waters,
Individuals yet intimately, intricately connected,
Blessed with the powers of heart, head, and hand
To steer our course.
Onward we travel,
Forward,
Always forward.
And as we reach the temporary shore of another evening
And shake off the grit of fears,
Doubts, and regrets, let us
Look up!
Up to the dark and profoundly beautiful
Face of the Universe that, in turn, smiles down upon us;
And may we remember that
Each one of us is known,
Is intended,
Is valued
By the Great and Eternal That Which Is.
Certain of this, let us welcome sleep
And the serenity it brings.
Let us place our weary heads upon softness and
Savor the peace, the stillness that is offered.
Then, when we awaken to the morning
Look up!
Up to the bright and beautifully brilliant
Face of Day,

And know that this moment is ours to
Do with as we will,
Sailing out, sailing on,
Individuals yet intricately, intimately connected,
Blessing one another with the powers of
Heart, head, and hand,
Steering our course forward,
Always forward.

For That Extra Night Every Four Years

May it be gentle,
Forgiving, compassionate,
This dark, tender night.

Made in the USA
Lexington, KY
14 December 2014